The Human Resource Development Handbook

The Human Resource Development Handbook

Pat Hargreaves and Peter Jarvis

KOGAN
PAGE

First published in 1998
Revised edition 2000

Kogan Page Limited
120 Pentonville Road
London NI 9JN
UK

Stylus Publishing Inc
22883 Quicksilver Drive
Sterling, VA 20166–2012
USA

British Library Cataloguing in Publication Data

A CIP record for this book is available from the British Library.

ISBN 0 7494 3223 3

Typeset by JS Typesetting, Wellingborough, Northants
Printed and bound in Great Britain by Biddles Ltd, Guildford and King's Lynn

Contents

PART 4 OCCUPATION OF HRD PROFESSIONALS

Preface

Aims of the book

This book is designed as a quick and easy-to-use manual for:

- staff developers
- health and safety officers
- welfare officers
- line managers who have a special responsibility for staff development
- all staff who are concerned with HRD.

This book is intended to provide a quick reference guide to the practicalities of work in staff development. We have brought together material from a variety of sources in a systematic fashion. The manual will provide:

- insight into the numerous roles of training providers
- an understanding of the skills and expertise needed to be a trainer
- information about the systems and processes of training, eg assessment of needs, formulation of objectives, the design, implementation and evaluation of training programmes
- practical advice about training
- help in order to avoid some of the pitfalls involved when providing a total training programme
- information for managers of human resources about the skills and personal qualities required by trainers and line managers.

The book is divided into four parts:

1. Human resource development (HRD) in the organization: learning and training
2. The roles of human resource (HR) developers
3. The training function
4. Occupation of HRD professionals.

We have tried to write the book so that each section can stand alone. Part 1 provides background information about HRD, organizations and the importance of the staff developer. We have separated the theoretical aspects of the staff developer's roles in Part 2 from the practical aspects of actually organizing and implementing the training function (Part 3). Part 4 is concerned with the staff developer's roles in educational guidance and also the occupation of the staff developer. There are many ways of undertaking the various roles and tasks involved in training activities, and we cannot hope to include every last detail but we have provided references for your additional reading at the end of each chapter. We hope that you will find the handbook useful and interesting.

PART 1

Human resource development (HRD) in the organization: learning and training

Chapter 1

The importance of the staff developer

This manual is intended to be useful as a quick day-to-day guide for busy people:

- HRD specialists
- line managers
- training managers
- staff developers
- health and safety officers
- welfare officers
- instructors
- trainers.

Each of these practitioners is regularly involved in the training and development of staff. In this handbook the concept 'staff developer' is used generically and includes all human resource development (HRD) practitioners as listed above since they all have education and training functions in their organizations.

Importance of work-based learning to organizations

Learning is the basis both of individual development and of organizational enhancement of education and training. The skills, knowledge and experience of each individual contribute to the economic growth of organizations, communities and nations. Such valuable human talent can be thought of in terms of human capital and is one of the primary requirements for national economic development. Not only do people make an economic contribution, they make a human one, a point we should never forget in the frenzy of organizational demands.

It has been found that in the United Kingdom some organizations spend approximately between 1 and 2 per cent of their salary bill on formal training for staff (Brewster and Hegewisch, 1994; Hargreaves, 1995). It has been estimated that in the United States, formal training in the workplace also accounts for approximately between 1 and 2 per cent of employers' salary bills and that work-based learning and formal education have accounted for at least two-thirds of the nation's productivity improvements since 1929. In addition, informal education and training 'at the work-bench' or 'desk' (which is difficult to define) may account for about six times the amount spent on formal training (Carnevale *et al.*, 1990). The US historian, Kett (1994) has suggested that by the start of the 1980s, the corporate training bill stood at over US$60 billion per annum!

As a result of such high investment in training and the promotion and integration of learning, organizations can expect to have the skills to remain innovative and competitive and to produce products and information of excellence. Staff developers, therefore, occupy a strategic role in the development of organizations and their capacity to operate in contemporary society.

Importance of work-based learning to people

Staff. developers and other professionals promote the continued training and education of the employed, the under-employed and the unemployed so as to:

- ensure that people are literate
- provide a highly skilled and flexible workforce
- provide opportunities for technological updating
- provide efficient managers and directors
- ensure that staff are able to develop their careers
- promote creativity and technological development within the workforce
- retrain staff who possess skills which are becoming obsolete
- promote the return of the unemployed to work.

Training is a growth industry which will continue into the foreseeable future, but it must keep pace with the requirements of employing organizations (see Perelman, 1984). In a fast developing world, technological development is rapid and knowledge and the skills and expertise held by the workforce can fast become obsolete. For example, it has been estimated that the half-life of education in terms of knowledge and skills required by software engineers may be about 2.5 years because the pace of technological development in this and other fields is moving so rapidly. The training department within an organization is effectively responsible for providing the workforce with a great deal of its up-to-date knowledge and skills, for promoting creativity and for helping the workforce towards a common goal – as defined by the organization's mission statement. In fact, it has a great deal of influence on what is learned in the 'corporate classroom' (see Marsick and Watkins, 1990).

The work of staff developers

Training provision in an organization may be wholly arranged by the training department (centralized) or some formal training may be arranged by departments or units (decentralized). The latter type more usually applies to technological specialized training. Whatever the situation, the training department in an organization has to plan, organize, implement, evaluate and record numerous types of formal and informal training initiatives and all of this has to be done in a cost-effective way. Depending on the size of the employing organization, staff developers will often be required to do the following:

- discuss strategic business and training plans with management teams or directors
- act as training consultants
- make training decisions
- plan and co-ordinate staff development activities according to staff and organizational needs (including health and safety initiatives)
- act as catalysts for training and learning
- provide a focal point for learning activities
- provide training-related communication channels between various levels of staff and management within the organization
- design training events
- support staff involved in external or distance learning schemes.

Staff developers often take responsibility for the whole training department, deciding on the resources to be made available for staff education and training, eg a resource centre, a library or computers for training. Sometimes training initiatives will be organized in-house either at the workbench or desk or by means of internally run or externally run courses or other initiatives.

Successful staff developers

The main requirements for successful staff developers include:

- possession of managerial and training skills
- ability to organize events

- ability to manage a complex social role
- fitting into the organizational culture (see Pettigrew *et al.*, 1982).

Like any other job, the staff developer's performance will depend on the manner in which they incorporate their own role expectations and personality into the culture of the organization where they are employed and conform to the expectations of management. It will also depend on the level of support provided by management. Staff developers often find that their role within the organization becomes a working compromise between how they wish to undertake their job and what is expected of them by management. Sometimes they may act as a 'provider of training', simply matching training needs with supply. At other times, they may plan, design and implement a whole series of training events so as to improve the capabilities of managers, ie communication between departments. Indeed, we suggest that they often 'walk a tightrope' in their efforts to get things done.

HRD professionals fall broadly into different groups depending on how they go about their work. Such groups are flexible, equally efficient and include the following descriptive categories:

- provider
- training manager
- change agent
- passive provider
- role-in-transition.

For further description, see Pettigrew *et al.* (1982).

Providers offer training that is designed to support organizational performance rather than to make great changes. They maintain neutrality and stability and do not seek to 'rock the boat' or to bring about great changes. Essentially, they treat all interest groups (eg staff and managers) as equal, whether representatives of top management, unions, or shop floor.

Training managers are concerned with the supervision and performance of the staff junior to them and manage the training policy and function rather than making training presentations.

Change agents are normally well qualified, experienced and work closely with top management. Usually they are concerned with changing an organization's culture, eg changing a hierarchical organization into one that has an open and flatter structure. These training practitioners are sometimes reactive (eg reacting to problems), while others are pro-active in that, in conjunction with management, they create change that they hope will be of benefit to the organization (see Boydell, 1990).

Passive providers of training services are concerned with the maintenance of training within the organization rather than making major changes. They may be passive in the sense that they are reactive rather than proactive, often refraining from exerting any influence on top management and waiting for individuals to come to them for help. They can suffer from lack of confidence.

Some staff developers do not fit into any of the above categories but having worked as a 'provider' recognize that they could make a wider impact if they became a specialist, eg a change agent. So they may alter the way in which they work, ie they enact a *role-in-transition*.

Some staff developers are employed only part-time and they may combine this with several other roles – perhaps as line manager or administration officer. In this instance, they tend to organize other specialists to run courses, as their time is limited.

Whatever the way in which staff developers decide to manage their job, they need to co-operate fully with the management team and maintain credibility with all staff. They have to be well organised and well qualified for the job, managing it efficiently and communicating clearly with all interest groups. Successful practitioners tend to adopt an informal proactive style, often wandering about the workplace and talking to people regularly about their training needs. Many also maintain a neutral position between staff and their managers. For example, on the one hand, they may be seen by staff as welfare officers and careers advisors, while on the other, they may be treated as confidants by directors and line managers. It is important that staff developers should maintain confidentiality and at the same time do their best for all the individuals in the organization and for the organization as a whole. If staff developers are too passive and lack interpersonal skills and expertise, they may find it difficult to maintain credibility and to get the support of managers and potential adult learners. If they are too active, they may alienate some useful support for their training programme.

In summary, a staff developer's role is about helping people to learn in all types of situation, but so far we have written very little about human resource development and organizations, how people learn and the factors which contribute to a good learning environment. These topics are addressed in the following chapters.

Staff development: education or training?

This is an age-old question but it still concerns purists. Some consider that these terms are synonymous, others think that they are different. However, in this handbook we have used the terms 'education' and 'training' synonymously for a number of reasons, which include the fact that there is no agreed definition of education nor of training and because we are more concerned with learning and the integrity of the individual. Additionally, it makes little sense for organizations to separate the 'training' aspect from that of 'education', since both may result in staff development, and employers are more concerned with the practicalities of meeting their organization's needs than they are with the niceties of academic argument. Indeed, Perelman (1984) points out that if broad-based literacy skills provided by general education are lacking, then traditional training programmes may fail. Thus, in practice these two concepts are inter-related.

The one distinction that we want to make is between these terms and indoctrination. We shall assume throughout this handbook that staff should not be indoctrinated, and that techniques that deny their autonomy are immoral and should not be employed.

Staff developers should:

• recognize the importance of work-based learning

• develop good managerial and organizational skills

• work to maintain credibility with the management team and with staff.

References and Further Reading

Boydell, TH (1990) *A Guide to the Identification of Training Needs*, (2nd edn), BACIE, London.

Brewster, C and Hegewisch, A (eds) (1994) *Policy and Practice in European Human Resource Management*, London, Routledge.

Carnevale, AP, Gainer, LJ and Villet, J (1990) *Training in America: The Organizaion and Strategic Role of Training*, Jossey-Bass, San Francisco.

Hargreaves, PM (1995) *The Training Officer: A Cost-effective Role in a Science Research Organisation?*, unpublished PhD thesis, University of Surrey.

Kett, JF (1994) *The Pursuit of Knowledge Under Difficulties: From Self-Improvement to Adult Education in America 1750–1990*, Stanford University Press, Stanford, CA and London.

Marsick, VJ and Watkins, KE (1990) *Informal and Incidental Learning in the Workplace*, Routledge, London.

Perelman, LJ (1984) *The Learning Enterprise: Adult Learning, Human Capital and Economic Development*, The Council on State Planning Agencies, Washington, DC.

Pettigrew, AM, Jones, GR and Reason, PW (1982) *Training and Development Roles in their Organisational Setting*, Manpower Services Commission Training Division, London.

Chapter 2

The concept of human resource development

As they work in a highly technological society, companies have to learn to adapt to rapid changes, to produce high quality goods and also to develop new products to remain competitive in the global market place. Strategic planning, forecasting of economic and demographic trends, job planning, training and care of their staff lie at the heart of this. Most organizations view human resource management as an investment in that it presents a way to integrate business plans and human skills so as to achieve its goals in terms of economic growth, products or services. In turn, the staff also gain in terms of remuneration, opportunities for learning and career development. This chapter provides a brief overview of some of the main issues that concern human resource development (HRD). Human resource development is precisely what it says it is – a process of helping individuals develop to their full potential – although the question remains as to for what ends.

First, we shall outline some of the concepts linked to human resource management and then move on to the history of human resource development. Finally, we outline the opportunities for learning in the workplace.

Human resource development

Within organizations there are broad areas concerned with human resources, that include the following:

- organization development linked to staff development
- job descriptions
- staff planning and recruitment
- staff benefits

- industrial relations, eg working with the trade unions
- training and development.

Most people in the management team, staff developers, line managers and staff themselves all have a part to play to ensure that HRD is successful. Periodic evaluation of human resource management systems is undertaken by organizations to ensure that the procedures work and are workable. If there are discrepancies in terms of low output, lack of trained staff, or high sickness rates, then the strategy may have to be altered. Some aspects of HRD are shown in Figure 2.1 and are discussed separately.

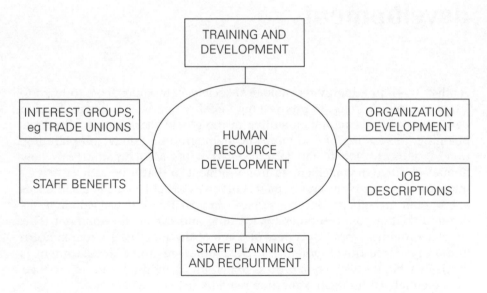

Figure 2.1   *Some of the main aspects of human resource development*

Organization development

Organizational development (OD) is the way in which people are managed and organized in order to get jobs done. Often it involves a gradual change in structure, eg updating a department or creating a new one, buying new equipment, or it may involve a change in culture that may lead to faster problem-solving in a more open and relaxed atmosphere. Whatever the changes, they usually involve staff who will often be consulted about new work procedures and about any training required. OD is discussed further in Chapter 3.

Job descriptions

All employing organizations plan their workload in terms of undertakings or projects that need to be completed if they are to achieve their goals. For example, these may include manufacturing a given number of cars for export, producing research data or simply teaching people. For each project to be completed, a number of jobs have to be done by people who have the skills to complete the many tasks involved. These may be managers, salespersons, computer programmers, instructors, etc. Before staff can be employed, the personnel department needs to have a description of each job so that it can recruit people with the appropriate qualifications, knowledge and skills. Job descriptions usually include information about tasks that need to be done, the performance standards required and a broad outline of the knowledge, skills and attitudes necessary to undertake each task.

Staff planning and recruitment

Personnel planning is linked to business strategies, a forecast of economic events, national demographic trends and the seniority and age of the existing workforce. It involves matching people to jobs, eg if an organization has a large number of middle managers nearing retirement within five years or so, it might decide either to recruit young graduates to train in order to fill their jobs, or to promote people from the existing workforce. Whatever the decision, it has to be taken well in advance and the position reviewed regularly in the light of new contracts or new projects. In conditions of economic decline involving job losses, there may be a readily available supply of staff to be recruited but these will need to have the right qualifications for the job or be willing to undertake appropriate training. On the other hand, if the national economy is buoyant and the national employment rate is high, then there may be a dearth of people to recruit. The personnel department has to weigh up the situation and recruit the best people it can for the remuneration offered.

Once individuals are recruited, their progress at work is usually monitored. Some people will want to establish a long-term career with the organization. Others may prefer to stay only a short while just to gain money or experience but whatever happens, they will probably be subject to appraisal.

The main purpose of appraisal is to help improve the performance of individuals, teams, divisions, departments or organizations as a whole. Appraisal should be an ongoing process of exchange of information between staff and managers of the appraisee's job performance. It should include an assessment of the following:

- performance of tasks
- management of staff
- financial management

- use of resources
- flexibility and potential for promotion.

This information is usually confirmed periodically, normally every six months to a year. At this time more formal assessments are made and forward job planning may occur. Not all organizations have forward job plans but if they are used they are often linked to an individual's promotion prospects and aspirations. Generally, they encourage personal responsibility and provide a framework that provides staff with a clear idea of what is expected of them. In turn, staff often provide some input to the plan. Often at this time staff may request training so as to undertake particular tasks and it is the responsibility of the staff developer and the line manager jointly to ensure that such requests are met.

Career development involves career planning (mainly by the individual and her/his line manager). Staff developers may promote career development of staff by providing relevant training initiatives to help them in their work and by acting as neutral interventionists in training-related disputes between line managers and their staff.

Staff benefits, industrial relations and interest groups

Staff benefits are usually arranged by the personnel department and can include basic remuneration and reimbursement of costs incurred during the course of work, eg travel costs. Benefits may also include subsidized meals or healthcare. Some staff view opportunities for training as a benefit, particularly as it is usually paid for by the employer or is subsidized. There are various interest groups concerned with staff benefits at work, including trade unions. The latter will ensure, for example, that statutory regulations on minimum pay are adhered to and they also help to monitor health and safety procedures. Often organizations provide accommodation and facilities for meetings with union representatives so as to promote good working relations and to settle work-related disputes.

Training and development of staff

In a dynamic organization, staff development is a regular and ongoing process that will be initiated by the employer or a professional body. From the description of human resource areas above it is clear that training and development of staff are linked to almost every aspect of human resource management. Staff developers play a vital role in assisting in the creation and development of their company as a learning organization. They may organize, or take part in, any educational or training initiative designed to enable individual employees to achieve their full potential. They are the advocates of training and development and sometimes have to persuade management that money spent on training and development is a good company invest-ment and that well-educated, efficient and forward-thinking creative staff will help organizations to establish themselves as producers of excellence. Staff developers also have a commitment to help in the development of structures and communication systems that will enable the company to develop and harness the expertise of staff in order both to produce end products of high quality and to remain ahead in the development of new commodities. In return, staff should receive opportunities for education and development and be able to look forward to successful careers.

Before moving on to discuss organizations in more detail in the next chap-ter, we shall look briefly at the history of staff training and discuss employee learning.

An historical overview of staff training

There are certain benchmarks in the history of the development of training activities and these may be summarized as:

- employee skilfulness
- employee efficiency
- employee satisfaction
- employee enhancement.
  (see Pace *et al.*, 1991.)

Various authors including Pace *et al.* (1991) provide an excellent summary of such historical developments. Until about the beginning of the nineteenth century, employee skilfulness was developed by informal methods with employees viewed as family members and producers, rather than as members of a workforce. During the next few decades until about the 1920s, employees were looked upon primarily as producers, with the result that employers focused attention on improving their efficiency, often with little concern for them as persons. Gradually, during the mid-twentieth century, emphasis on employee satisfaction increased which, incidentally, probably also contributed to employee efficiency. Finally, this was superseded by employee enhancement – an approach which continues to the present day. Now, education and training are holistic; development of individuals as persons is considered to be important, not only for its own sake but also for reasons of organizational efficiency and national economy. Trainers are, therefore, concerned with human learning in all its complexity.

Employee learning

In general, people are interested in learning something new. Research undertaken during the 1970s showed that approximately 90 per cent of adults were engaged in self-managed learning projects of various kinds (Tough, 1979). While Tough's work was with a small sample, it did indicate that many of the self-managed learning episodes undertaken during people's leisure were actually vocationally orientated. Today, there is no indication that this situation has changed drastically. People learn from many different sources to help them acquire skills that can be used in leisure or at work. This is something managers have to recognize and, perhaps, try to reward.

Education and training initiatives based solely on formal learning opportunities are provided by employers, academic institutions, associations and societies, but these are not the only ways employees can learn. Numerous informal methods of learning are also available. For example, there are increasing opportunities for relatively inexpensive foreign travel, films, videos, books, magazines, newspapers, radio and television and the Internet. These all play a part in imparting knowledge to people world-wide.

HRD seeks to enhance the personal and work-related skills of individuals, helping them to achieve their full potential. Generally there are many different approaches to the way in which people learn at work, such as apprenticeship, day-release courses, mentoring-type schemes, self-managed learning, classroom teaching, etc.

Apprenticeship systems provide good examples of training at the bench or desk. These formal programmes combine practical work with theory that is often learned as part of a day-release programme at local colleges. Usually the apprentice staff member is supervised by experienced employees. It is a good system of learning but many trainees need encouragement to complete formal apprenticeships, which often involve external classes and homework, because of the amount of time involved. Some of the learning is more informal and it is this which is often called, in a derogatory fashion, 'sitting by Nellie'. In effect this informal method of learning can be very useful provided that the instructors are experienced and good at helping people to learn.

Employers sometimes offer day-release courses for staff to attend colleges, universities and the organization's own training establishments. Day-release is a common feature in training (see Killeen and Bird, 1981, for an early study of paid educational leave).

In recent years, a competency-based system to obtain National Vocational Qualifications (NVQs), involving work-based learning, has been introduced and, where this occurs, staff are often assigned to a senior colleague who can help prepare them for their tests. Sometimes these are called mentoring systems, although these systems may be little different to the original apprenticeship systems. There are, however, other mentoring systems in which staff are assigned for several months or a year to a more experienced and senior staff member. This often applies to administrators or managers.

As we have shown, there are a variety of forms of training, all of which concern the staff developer. Even these already discussed might be argued by some to be termed either education or training. However, they are all about learning which is why we wish to avoid the rather crude distinction between the former two terms. They are all part of what is now coming to be seen as lifelong learning, although the staff developer's job is technically closer to providing opportunities for continuing education than lifelong learning! Work-based and non-work-based learning can complement each other and should help employees or potential employees to enhance their own potential.

In conclusion, HRD specialists are quite central to the production of a culture in the organization that motivates and enables personnel to achieve their potential and gain a high level of job satisfaction. They are also important to the way that departments and groups succeed in co-ordinating staff effort. In the next chapter we shall discuss organizations.

Staff developers should:

- recognize that there are many aspects to human resource management and that human resource development impinges on most areas at work

- recognize that helping people to learn has the potential to help both the individual and the employer

- understand that they have a responsibility to ensure that staff training and development happen.

References and Further Reading

French, W and Bell, C (1984) *Organization Development: Behavioral Science Interventions for Organizational Improvement*, (3rd edn), Prentice-Hall, Englewood Cliffs, NJ and London.

Gutteridge, TG (1986), Organizational career development systems, in Hall, DT and Associates (eds), *Career Development in Organizations*, Jossey-Bass, San Francisco pp. 50–62.

Killeen, J and Bird, M (1981) *Education and Work: A Study of Paid Educational Leave in England and Wales* (1974–7), National Institute of Adult Education, Leicester.

Pace, RW, Smith, PC and Mills, GE (1991) *Human Resource Development: The Field*, Prentice-Hall, Englewood Cliffs, NJ.

Tough, A (1979) *The Adult's Learning Projects* (2nd edn), The Ontario Institute For Studies in Education, Ontario.

Watkins, K (1991) Many voices: defining human resource development from different disciplines, *Adult Education Quarterly*, 41(4): 241–55.

Chapter 3

Organizations and development

Organizations are 'a type of collectivity established for the pursuit of specific aims or goals, characterised by a formal structure of rules, authority relations, a division of labour and limited membership or admission' *(Collins Dictionary of Sociology*, 1991). They include commercial companies, research institutions, government departments, academic institutions and non-profit-making concerns, such as charities. They range from small businesses with only several employees to vast multinational, commercial companies which employ many thousands of people. Organizations are expected to be efficient at producing high quality goods, products or services, to remain up to date with technology, to satisfy customers and provide a safe working environment. They contribute to economic and socio-economic growth, or knowledge at the national or international level.

This chapter has four main sections: the first examines organizational structure, the second looks at the way that organizations develop, the third briefly looks at the staff developer's role within the organization and, finally, we shall examine health and safety at work.

Structure of organizations

Organizations have a variety of different structures, depending upon their size, their aims and their management philosophy. Various models have been devised to explain the managerial structure of organizations, such as the one described by Handy (1985) who suggests that the culture of organizations is broadly oriented to:

- task
- power

17

- person
- role.

Task culture is job-oriented. Here, emphasis is on having people, groups or teams with the expertise to get things done. Thus joint effort is important and groups or teams are often empowered to make major decisions. On the other hand, they may be disbanded or reformed, depending on requirements, to get the next task completed.

Power culture emphasizes influence and trust in individuals who are often judged on results. In this example, individuals tend to fill key posts and may be entrepreneurial and are prepared to take risks. Heads of groups are independent but generally there is little bureaucracy.

Person culture is based on a concept that the structure exists mainly to serve the people within it. Those people usually work in their areas of particular expertise but may find it easy to take their specialist knowledge to other employment. Role culture emphasizes procedures and job descriptions rather than one person or one task. The allocation of work is based on a division of labour but may be slow to react to change.

Handy (1985) gives examples of different management structures, some formal and hierarchical, others formal but non-hierarchical and yet others as informal and entrepreneurial. Within a strong hierarchical structure there will usually be several layers of management with a top-down management style. Other organizations may have a flatter, less centralized, lateral management structure that usually makes it easier for staff of all grades to communicate with each other. There is certainly a movement at present to cut down on the number of layers and to create flatter organizations.

Within any organizational structure, work groups will be organized according to the company's ethos and in accord with the types of work undertaken. Whatever the structure, groups of people tend to work in teams, sometimes within departments, developing and learning as they proceed. Their activities must be co-ordinated by departmental heads, project managers and line managers in such a way that projects can be completed efficiently. Large successful organizations need systems and procedures in order to achieve this, but these also need to be flexible so that people can be innovative and achieve their own potential. Too much top-down management and too many bureaucratic procedures inhibit innovation and consequently tend to curtail staff growth and development.

In organizations, especially the larger ones, there is a need for managers to exercise a concern for the employees and while there may be human resource generalists and specialists, ie training managers, staff developers, welfare officers, health and safety officers, all line managers also have this responsibility. In many ways, employees are the greatest resource a company has, so that such positions are very important if organizations are to maximize their capacity. The culture of the organization is important not only to individuals but also to the organization itself.

All employees, whatever their grade and whether they are professionals or not, contribute to the culture of the organization. We have seen that they may possess abilities and talents that will enable them to fit into the organization and empower it, partly as a result of socialization, but they may need assistance from others, such as the HRD specialist, in order to learn the skills that will enable them to play their part in the team or group or department, etc.

In some instances, however, staff may be restricted in their behaviour due to management structure or company policy. In these instances, it may be the job of the HRD specialist to advise the management team about the outcomes of its policies. However, there are other reasons why people adopt the stance that they do, and it is wise for HRD specialists to understand these if they can.

Unions can also play a part in creating this culture, since they are in a position to provide the workforce with information designed to influence its decisions about work practices, etc. Staff developers need, therefore, to communicate regularly with trades union officers.

Organization development (OD)

Most people look upon organization development (OD) as the way in which an organization is managed in terms of individual and task processes, ie getting jobs done. Some researchers look upon it as a way of improving the climate of an organization, linked to its mission, so as to ensure that the goals of the organization and its staff are compatible. Others regard OD as involving a change in structure or a change in culture applicable at the working group or department level that may improve an organization's problem-solving and updating processes (see French and Bell, 1984).

Organizational development occurs through strategies that implement ways of working, relating to factors such as resources, pace of working, strengths, weaknesses, and criteria for standards and quality. Processes are also examined in terms of learning and problem-solving, innovation, change, work procedures and output. Gradual changes will occur often under the guidance of HRD professionals, but the most effective changes occur through collaborative efforts on the part of management and staff. Often the reasons for change are the need to improve the quality and range of products and to improve the efficiency of the production process through good team-working and problem-solving throughout the various levels of the organization.

Kay (1990) suggests that there is no single best approach to the management problems facing staff. As we saw in Chapter 1, sometimes qualified 'change agents' may intervene as facilitators and help groups of staff in organizations to change their attitudes or ways of working, in order to improve output and quality (see London, 1988).

Organization development cannot occur without staff development. Within an organization, education and training may be centralized and run from a central co-ordinating point, or be decentralized so that decisions about training are made at the department, group or unit level. For example, managerial training may be arranged centrally but skills training may be arranged wholly by, say, engineering or computing departments mainly for their own staff. Generally, centralized training occurs where there is a need to implement change or to address new innovations throughout the workplace, while decentralization occurs to fit the purposes of departments or individuals.

HRD strategy by top management should incorporate a planned sequence of learning opportunities for staff. This preferred approach implies that HRD training practitioners, such as staff developers, should be invited periodically to attend meetings to discuss the total business plan and the needs for recruitment and training.

A major responsibility of staff developers within organizations is to encourage both senior management and also the rest of the workforce in promoting a 'learning' culture, so that everyone is happy to become involved in learning to undertake new tasks. This leads to a flexible workforce. Denial of access to training may lead to low morale of staff and, ultimately, to low productivity. The staff developer should ensure that equal opportunities for training occur, regardless of class, gender or age (as discussed further in Chapter 4).

We have seen that staff development is usually linked to appraisal and career development. As staff are effectively a 'captive audience', there must be opportunities for personal and vocational development and career advancement at a level broadly similar to, or better than, that experienced by staff in other organizations.

The staff developer in the organization

Staff developers bring their own personalities, values, attitudes and knowledge to their job. When these fit in with the culture of the organization, it often means that staff developers get a great deal of satisfaction from their work. Staff developers have to ensure that their behaviour is acceptable to the culture of the organization as a whole. They need to determine, from the outset, what the management team expects and they must publicize and discuss the wide range of training initiatives in which staff are able to participate. At the same time, they should be advocates for the staff with the management in respect of all forms of personal training and development. Staff developers have both formal and informal roles to play within the organization in order to ensure that they can represent all interests in the organization to the benefit of the whole.

Boundary management is a significant aspect of the staff developer's role. It is important to note that understanding and managing boundaries can play a crucial part in the promotion of the power, legitimacy and credibility of the training department. Staff developers need to build up good relationships with all staff, not least in order to acquire resources, exchange services and also to discover training needs.

Health and safety at work

Most managers and supervisors in organizations are now aware of their legal obligations as far as health and safety is concerned. For example, European Union legislation (1992) requires employers to establish safety at work, to provide staff with literature and/or specialized training-awareness lectures on selected health and safety topics. Employers must ensure that working practices do not result in injury to staff. For example, health and safety regulations include a requirement for employers to implement the following procedures:

- Assess computer visual display units (VDUs) for health hazards.
- Ensure that people working with VDUs are not subject to eye strain or repetitive strain injury.
- Control the use and storage of toxic chemicals (COSHH).
- Ensure the general safety of all electrical and mechanical equipment.
- Ensure that noise levels are within acceptable standards.
- Transport materials, gases and liquids safely.
- Provide protective equipment or clothing.
- Ensure safe manual handling.
- Undertake risk assessment on a wide range of work situations.

For a full list of the requirements see the approved code of practice (Health and Safety Executive, 1992 and updated in 1997).

Individual staff and managers have a health and safety responsibility towards their colleagues and they should be aware of the regulations and their responsibilities. Staff developers and health and safety officers should obtain up-to-date copies of health and safety regulations so that they can organize training events for managers, staff and colleagues. Usually it is best for well-qualified health and safety advisors to provide courses. There are now formal qualifications for health and safety officers, including National Vocational Qualifications in Health and Safety and higher degree courses.

Staff developers should:

- talk to managers and staff to define how each group views the structure of the organization in which they work

- see a copy of the company's mission statement and its business plan

- ensure that they know what the management team expect of them

- maintain good relations with the local trade union officers

- remain aware of health and safety issues at work and know their responsibilities with respect to organizing the necessary training

- know what their own role is within the organization.

References and Further Reading

Argyris, C (1982) *Reasoning Learning and Action*, Jossey-Bass, San Francisco.
Collins (1991) *Dictionary of Sociology*, Collins, London.
French, W and Bell, C (1984) *Organization Development: Behavioral Science Interventions for Organizational Improvement*, (3rd edn), Prentice-Hall, Englewood Cliffs, NJ.
Goldstein, IL (1980) Training in work organizations, *Annual Review of Psychology*, 31, 229–72.
Handy, CB (1985) *Understanding Organizations*, (3rd edn), Penguin, Harmondsworth.
Health and Safety Executive (1992; 1997) *Management of Health and Safety at Work Regulations 1992*. HMSO, London.
Kay, R (1990) *Managing Creativity in Science and Hi-tech*, Springer-Verlag, New York.
London, M (1988) *Change Agents: New Roles and Innovation Strategies for Human Resource Professionals*, Jossey-Bass, San Francisco and London.
Pace, RW, Smith, PC and Mills, GE (1991) *Human Resource Development: The Field*, Prentice-Hall, Englewood Cliffs, NJ.
Stewart, V (1990) *The David Solution. How to Reclaim Power and Liberate your Organization*, Gower Publishing Co Ltd, Aldershot.
Stranks, J (1997) *A Manager's Guide to Health and Safety at Work*, (5th edn), Kogan Page, London.

Chapter 4

People development for the organization

As we saw in the previous chapters, HRD, as practised in organizations, seeks to enhance the personal and work-related skills of staff and to help them achieve their full potential. Its importance to the organization cannot be overstated. To achieve reputations as centres of excellence, organizations need to retain and retrain highly skilled and creative generalists and specialists.

There are various views regarding the extent that employer-led systems of training and development can benefit the individual. Marsick and Watkins (1990) emphasize that the benefits of employee training are vast, not only in terms of formal training and staff development initiatives, but also in terms of informal and incidental learning that occurs through work experience. Company training initiatives make a significant difference to the earning potential and the career prospects of staff. Versatile staff are more likely to adapt to change either within or outside the workplace. In this chapter, therefore, we outline some of the responsibilities that the organization has in employee development.

Equal opportunities

Most companies have equal opportunities policies, although, unfortunately, not all companies have implemented them. Discrimination may occur because of gender, age, marital status, race, ethnic origins or disability. Indeed, training opportunities may be discriminatory for certain sectors of the workforce. For example, in some countries, women receive disproportionately less company training than men, and the economically disadvantaged often receive least of all (Marsick and Watkins, 1990). Furthermore, there may be age-related differences in training opportunities as levels of training for older workers may depend on the national economic situation and levels of unemployment. If staff are difficult to recruit, it may be advantageous for employers to train existing staff, whatever their age. On the other hand, if there are plenty of young people available for work, employers may take on new staff in preference to training those closer to retirement. It follows that the unemployed may also lose out on training.

While staff developers do not have the final word in the arrangements of all staff development, we have to remember that some groups have more opportunities, attend different locations for their training and gain better qualifications as a result, so that training is never equally provided for all employees. Staff developers do have some responsibility, however, to ensure that opportunities are as equally offered as possible regardless of age, gender or position. In the instance of disabled people, it may be necessary to provide special accommodation or facilities for courses.

How organizations help staff to achieve their full potential

Professionals are aware that recent rapid technological innovation has caused an increase in the likelihood of professional obsolescence which must be avoided by continuous learning. Staff, particularly professionals and other skilled staff, are accustomed to learning informally and formally using a number of different methods and employing many different sources, including local colleges, higher education institutes and other commercially orientated organizations. Professionals are also more aware of the opportunities for these types of development than many other grades, but staff developers do need to make other staff equally aware of the opportunities that their employers can provide for them.

Organizations need to undertake the following activities in order to help staff achieve their full potential and:

- promote equal learning opportunities for staff
- help staff to develop strategies to adapt to change
- promote creativity and innovation
- help create a learning culture in the organization.

Resources

It is important for staff developers to be aware of the need to provide all the basic resources for learning and development within the training centre, or area. These should include the following:

- computers, computing support staff and computer-assisted learning disks
- study areas with all necessary facilities
- noticeboards providing information about and access to formal and informal courses covering vocational and non-vocational topics
- allocation of a training budget or payment for courses, agreed previously with the management team and line managers
- well-equipped conference rooms (for large organizations)
- syndicate rooms
- all audio-visual aids, such as slide projector, screen, video recorder or player, television monitor, overhead projectors, flip charts, paper and pens
- photocopying facilities
- telephones, telex, facsimile
- library facilities.

Basic training provision

The training provision made by the organization will depend to a great extent upon the size and function of the organization, but will probably include the following types of course:

- health and safety procedures
- job training
- technological updating for specialists and specialist support staff
- team building and working with others
- courses on techniques for financial management for budget holders
- quality management and customer care programmes for all staff
- initiatives on strategic, project and personnel management for directors, managers and supervisors
- marketing and sales
- language training.

Sources of provision

Staff development initiatives may be conducted in-house, at external educational establishments or by open or distance learning and may be long term eg day-release or sabbatical courses, or short term. In-house provision can include:

- Learning at the workplace. These may be long-term or short-term activities ranging from single session informal training by colleagues at the bench or desk to formal long-term apprenticeships.
- Courses, seminars or workshops run on-site with various in-house staff or by external specialists. These may include a wide range of vocational topics, language or personal development topics.

- Self-help groups specializing in various topics, eg computing, statistics.
- Mentoring programmes and job or departmental exchange.

Examples of the types of vocational and non-vocational courses currently offered by external organizations are shown in Appendix A.

In addition, numerous specialist vocationally oriented technical and computing courses are also offered by external organizations. Although it is accepted that some adults learn best through experience and at the bench or desk rather than through highly structured courses, the latter are valuable in certain subject areas where large numbers of staff have to be trained to high standards, as for example in 'customer services' or some forms of computing.

Assistance from other staff

The cost-effectiveness of staff development can be helped greatly by the willingness of skilled staff to teach their colleagues. Remember that organizations may employ more personnel with knowledge and skills than appears on the surface. Many people have hidden talents! Staff developers might well be advised to make a list of people who are willing to share their specific skills with colleagues. The organization should also be prepared to offer a basic training in teaching adults for people who have, and are willing to share, such skills. Staff developers should also organize mentoring courses for those members of staff prepared to act in this capacity within the organization. However, the use of their time for training others has to be balanced with the requirement for them to get on with their own job. Staff may be less than happy about presenting such sessions as 'Health and Safety Awareness', and it is usually best to ask professional health and safety instructors or lecturers to provide these courses.

Increasing communication and co-operation between staff

It is clear that the need for good formal and informal communication channels is very important in creating an organization of excellence. Staff developers can do a great deal to facilitate this by:

- providing management training for most staff, even non-managers. This may help staff to view their own role and that of others with whom they work as more focused and organized. This will help to get the best out of staff. Some also find management courses helpful in giving feedback to their own line managers and in liaising and negotiating with colleagues
- promoting interpersonal effectiveness

- promoting teamwork among staff
- implementing interviewing and staff reporting courses for all staff, whatever their grade, in order to maintain a fair staff appraisal and career management system
- helping staff to understand the importance of personal communication and networking with others
- providing refresher courses in interpersonal skills and management training.

It is important for staff developers to be aware of how people actually learn, so Chapter 6 will provide an outline of the adult's learning processes. In the next chapter we discuss aspects of the learning organization.

Staff developers should:

- discuss with team managers, project managers and line managers the amount of time and funds which can be allocated to staff for education and training initiatives

- ensure that staff are aware that staff development initiatives are available to them

- regularly circulate details of free (and other) seminars, video sessions and courses

- encourage staff to participate in self-help groups

- ensure that adequate resources are provided.

References and Further Reading

Carnevale, AP (1984) *Jobs for the Nation: Challenge for a Society Based on Work*, American Society for Training and Development, Alexandria, VA.

Carnevale, AP (1986) The learning enterprise, *Training and Development Journal*, 40(1): 18–26.

Further Education Unit (1987) *Planning Staff Development: A Guide for Managers*, Further Education Unit, London.

Gutteridge, TG (1986) Organisational career development systems, in Hall, DT and Associates (eds), *Career Development in Organisations*, Jossey-Bass, London, pp. 50–62.

Institute of Personnel Management (1984) *Continuous Development: People and Work*, IPM, London.

Marsick, VJ (1987) (ed) *Learning in the Workplace*, Croom Helm, London.

Marsick, VJ and Watkins, KE (1990) *Informal and Incidental Learning in the Workplace*, Routledge, London.

Mayo, A (1991) *Managing Careers: Strategies for Organizations*, Institute of Personnel Management, London.

Payne, J (1991) *Women, Training and the Skills Shortage: The Case for Public Investment*, Policy Studies Institute, London.

Pearson, P and Heyno, A (1988) *Helping the Unemployed Professional*, John Wiley, Chichester.

Robinson, DG and Robinson, JC (1989) *Training for Impact: How to Link Training to Business Needs and Measure the Results*, Jossey-Bass, San Francisco.

Tough, A (1979) *The Adult's Learning Projects*, (2nd edn), The Ontario Institute For Studies in Education, Austin, Texas.

Chapter 5

The learning organization

The learning organization is 'one that learns continuously and transforms itself. Learning takes place in individuals, teams, the organisation, and even the communities with which the organisation interacts. Learning is a continuous, strategically used process' (Watkins and Marsick, 1993). Organizations must be learning organizations if they are to achieve excellence. They need continually to improve their products, data or services while also retaining and developing a highly skilled, innovative and motivated workforce. A learning organization seeks to improve its output and ways of working by continually improving its knowledge, understanding and practices. The basic concept is that it should adapt quickly to change and learn continually from its experiences, and that all people within such an organization should have a shared vision and purpose. The ethical and underlying social values of all the employees should be taken into account in this endeavour.

Among the main aims of the learning organization are:

- enabling staff to recognize problems early and take time to reflect on their underlying causes, so that they can be remedied
- considering new and innovative ideas about products and processes. These should also be discussed and incorporated as appropriate
- discussing difficult issues
- learning from the experiences of others.

Different people tend to have different views on how learning organizations actually operate. Various authors, eg Argyris (1982), Senge (1990), Easterby-Smith (1991), Watkins and Marsick (1993) have pointed out that such organizations take great care about the way in which they organize the following:

- structure and control, ensuring that the systems are relatively flat and not hierarchical

- leadership issues
- motivation and creativity of staff
- efficient communication and information systems
- organizational learning
- detection of problem areas and finding solutions
- use of technology in learning.

Structure and control

The main idea behind the learning organization is that openness, decentralization of control and a sense of freedom should operate. There are many examples of organizations that failed partly because they adopted a culture that promotes central controls and rigid procedures, resulting in managers being afraid to take risks and make mistakes. Consequently, they failed to learn from their own or others' experiences.

Senge (1990) suggests that an important component of such an organization is 'systems thinking' to help solve problems. This is based on the premise that the structure of an organization (or any system) influences events and the behaviour of people connected with it. Flexible systems will enable staff to be flexible, while too much control will stifle innovation and advancement. Learning organizations should offer staff opportunities to gain experience in several different ways within the organization.

At present, there is insufficient information on the extent to which personal or group factors determine a change agent's ability to 'turn around' organizations. Often managers responsible for turning around organizations are typically young, but not all mature managers seek to maintain the status quo – many are forward-thinking and creative. Experienced staff developers may be required to help in this process. Success will depend partly on their creative ability and on group interaction.

Leadership issues

Many learning organizations encourage managers to adopt good leadership strategies and help staff in their working groups to create a vision for future working practices. It may well be that leadership training is even more important for managers in learning organizations than almost any other form of staff development. Certainly, staff developers require some leadership skills as well.

Motivation and creativity of staff

In many organizations staff are expected to fit in with the internal culture, sometimes even to the extent of the way that they dress. However, this may be counter-productive. If managers are not flexible in outlook, or are too specialized, then the organization may become too narrowly focused and thus the motivation and creative thought, a necessary precursor to innovation, may be stifled. Furthermore, if people are to be creative, then they need to experiment, eg run pilot schemes for ways of working or for marketing products, etc. It follows that a learning organization must be flexible and have systems that reward successful innovation. However, inevitably, some ventures will fail, so that it is equally important that those who initiated them should not be penalized. On the other hand, it is accepted that such a philosophy has its limitations because successful organizations cannot accept repeated failure. A balance has to be sought between control of experimentation and freedom of staff.

Staff developers will sometimes be called upon to organize courses in 'creative thinking' so as to optimize the innovative capacity of staff. Such courses may be aimed at newly recruited staff who may be unsure as to what extent they are expected to be innovative. On the other hand, although individual ideas are important, strategies for teamworking are essential. Senge (1990) emphasizes that, if necessary, individuals should be motivated to work as part of a team, sharing a common vision of the direction in which they would like to see the organization develop, sharing experiences, and promoting 'openness' and dialogue within the team. Staff developers can promote teamworking by organizing team-building exercises, and courses on team interaction using methods such as open discussion, role play, problem-solving exercises, case studies and simulation. Such methods are discussed further in Chapters 13 and 15.

Qualified staff developers may be asked to counsel managers and staff. Rather than solve problems for individuals, the latter should be helped to reach their own solutions. Often training specialists may be helpful in promoting the idea of openness, encouraging staff and managers to discuss their successes and failures. (Counselling is discussed further in Chapters 10 and 18.)

Efficient communication and information systems

Learning organizations need good communication and information systems in order to promote the learning culture. Staff developers should endeavour to ensure that systems of openness are in operation and they should organize courses that promote good communication. They should also ensure that staff are confident that their views and ideas will be considered.

Managers in all learning organizations need to be fully aware of total and departmental output in terms of the following:

- qualifications of each member of staff
- the quality and quantity of products
- data and services
- marketing statistics
- financial accounts.

Learning organizations not only keep such accurate up-to-date statistics, they also remain closely in contact with their customers in order to be able to forecast their needs, adapt their production and keep ahead of competitors. Ideally, communication channels should ensure a free flow of information to anyone who needs to know what is happening throughout the organization. Argyris (1982) argues that because of faulty ideas and values inherited by individuals in cultural and socialization processes, they may experience problems particularly in communication and problem-solving.

Organizational learning

Organizational learning arises from individual and collective formal and informal learning within an organization. As discussed in Chapter 2, learning may occur as an 'at the bench or desk' experience, or because of other informal or formal courses, seminars or other initiatives. Organizational learning may take place as a result of individual learning, provided that individuals are willing to share their learning with others and that there are efficient communication channels within the organization that enable them to do so. Such action learning is promoted if individuals work on real problem-solving situations – reflecting and learning from their experiences (see McGill and Beaty, 1992). The basic idea is that, as a result of their combined learning and open discussion, individuals will help the organization to innovate, remain up-to-date with new technology, develop high quality products and remain ahead of competitors. Team learning can also play a vital role in achieving this task.

Adults tend to learn best if there is some element of self-direction within the training and education curriculum. This self-direction might take the form of work-based projects, long-term research, academic inquiry or finding solutions to problems. This form of staff development may run in parallel with other formal or non-formal initiatives.

In addition to the intentional learning gained by staff, there is also unintentional or incidental learning gained as a by-product of informal or formal intentional learning. Sometimes this incidental information may result in staff developing solutions to problems or in completing tasks more efficiently.

However, staff may remain tacit about incidental learning and may not pass it on to others for a variety of reasons. For example, they may lack the confidence to suggest new ways of doing things or they may feel constrained by existing organizational procedures.

Staff developers and managers should seek to harness all types of individual formal, informal and incidental learning by promoting dialogue and exchange of views between individuals, teams or groups and departments. Thus, the organization may then reap the benefit of everyone's experiences. Consequently, it is important to promote a climate of trust between different members of staff. In addition, it should be recognized that sending individual staff on continuing education courses is of little value to the organization if it does not learn the lessons that the individual staff learned, so that there should always be opportunities to get feedback from continuing education courses and for departments and organizations to see if they need to adapt to and gain from the lessons learned on such courses.

Some forward-thinking organizations, such as Motorola, promote self-directed learning through autonomy and self-development. Some provide funds on a limited scale to enable staff to choose from a range of courses, which are not necessarily linked to the needs of the organization. In this way, they develop diversity within their workforce, which contributes to a highly skilled organization. For example, the Ford Motor Company of Dagenham have developed heavily subsidized student-centred training programmes in which employees are encouraged to participate. The organization usually pays the full cost of work-related courses, and at least 50 per cent of some non-work-related courses, eg some language courses. The success of this approach also provides evidence that staff are keen to take up educational opportunities made available to them by employers.

Recently, the Corporation of London Education Department has tried to foster a partnership with City firms by offering a voucher scheme in which the employees, the employers and the City share the costs of some forms of training (Jarvis *et al.*, 1997). Staff developers elsewhere might consider approaching adult education officers in Local Education Authorities to see what forms of partnership might be facilitated between their company and the LEA. Generally, corporate universities are playing an increasing role in staff development.

Detection of problem areas: finding solutions

Strategies need to be adopted that seek to detect the underlying cause of problems, often by reframing them so that they can be remedied. Argyris (1982) emphasizes tbat there is no organizational development without societal and cultural changes. Furthermore, he suggests that the way organizations control the activities of staff may inhibit an efficient approach to learning. He points out that many activities which are associated with excellence are very open – with staff and managers discussing organizational problems. He stresses the importance of the 'double-loop' process of learning, seeing it as a way to increase the ability of individuals within the organization to find solutions by problematizing the problem situation, which enables the staff to get at the faulty underlying values, policies and practices seemingly inherent not only in the individuals themselves but also within the organization.

Such 'double-loop' procedures are seen as a way of solving not only the symptoms but remedying the underlying condition(s) which cause the initial problem. By contrast, a 'single-loop' learning system, used to solve the problem itself, only solves the surface problem and rarely tackles the underlying causes, so that the problems may recur. Argyris suggests that for double-loop learning to be genuine, major changes need to be made to the organizational learning system.

One major set of problems that occurs in organizations is the way that staff perceive other employees and the way that their perceptions control their behaviour. In the 1970s, for example, Argyris and his colleagues suggested that adults tend to make sweeping generalizations about others, which both encourage feelings of being threatened and affect behaviour. Senge (1990) elaborates on this by suggesting that our minds move at 'lightning speed' so that we fail to observe accurately, but still form 'mental models' from which we make erroneous assumptions about others, based on these generalizations, which we then assume to be reality. For example, during their day-to-day activities, staff may make false assumptions that boundaries exist between themselves and colleagues or within working groups. Such assumptions may affect the way that they work and may affect their interpersonal relationships. Staff may also be afraid to question the existence of seemingly long-drawn-out procedures. For this reason openness in an organization should be promoted so as to help staff to voice their problems and in instances such as these, the staff developer can have a major role.

While it is acknowledged that all organizations need some form of control in the way in which procedures are undertaken and in the performance of staff, this control needs to be enabling rather than inhibiting (Stewart, 1990). Too much control inhibits good performance. It is for this reason that many organizations have introduced the idea of performance objectives. These are set by mutual agreement between reporting officers and their staff. Often staff appraisals are based on whether such targets have been attained. In this way, staff have some method of regulating their workload and appraisals.

Use of technology in learning

Computers are a major source of information, particularly with the development of the Internet and computer-assisted learning programmes. Organizations may go one step further in developing software to simulate future events. Senge (1990) coined the word 'microworlds', using it partly in the context of computer-based models for team and business interaction. Staff developers need to ensure that there is both availability of up-to-date computers and software and that staff have the ability to use them effectively. It is not by accident that the term 'computer illiteracy' is becoming more common. Some firms such as the Xerox Corporation provide staff with simulations of what may happen in the future to enable them to envisage future problems or opportunities (see also Jones and Hendry, 1994).

Trainer input

From the above discussion about learning organizations, it can be seen that staff developers have a major input to make. They may be able to increase flexibility by organizing job rotation or mentoring programmes, so that staff can gain experience. It is sometimes best to ask people within the organization to train others rather than using outside consultants. They may be able to affect the culture of the organization by the courses that they provide, in the way that they assist in the redesign of the work and in the way through which they facilitate communication channels.

So far we have said very little about how people learn and the factors which contribute to a good learning environment. These topics are addressed in the following chapter.

Staff developers should:

- promote the maintenance of good communication pathways throughout the organization

- retain a neutral stance between staff and managers

- facilitate training in leadership

- promote the idea of 'openness'

- encourage staff to discuss problems with their managers, and vice versa

- provide staff with information technology for learning

- put forward the idea of a staff 'suggestions scheme' for long-term or short-term improvements to ways of working.

References and Further Reading

Argyris, C (1982) *Reasoning, Learning and Action,* Jossey-Bass, San Francisco.

Argyris, C and Schon, DA (1974) *Theory in Practice: Increasing Professional Effectiveness,* Jossey-Bass, San Francisco.

Easterby-Smith, M (1991) Creating a learning organisation, *Personal Review* 19: 24–8.

Jarvis, P, Holford, J and Griffin, C (1997) *Towards the Learning City,* Corporation of London Education Department, London.

Jones, AM and Hendry, C (1994) The learning organization: adult learning and organizational transformation, *British Journal of Management,* 5: 153–62.

Kay, R (1990) *Managing Creativity in Science and Hi-tech,* Springer-Verlag, New York.

Marsick, VJ and Watkins, K (1990) *Informal and Incidental Learning in the Workplace,* Routledge, London.

McGill, I and Beaty, L (1992) *Action Learning: A Practitioner's Guide,* Kogan Page, London.

Senge, PM (1990) *The Fifth Discipline: The Art and Practice of the Learning Organisation,* Doubleday, New York.

Stewart, V (1990) *The David Solution: How to Reclaim Power and Liberate your Organisation,* Gower Publishing Co Ltd, Aldershot.

Watkins, K and Marsick, V (1993) *Sculpting the Learning Organisation Lessons in the Art and Science of Systematic Change,* Jossey-Bass, San Francisco.

Chapter 6

The learning process

Throughout these early chapters we have emphasized that the staff developer's role is about helping staff to learn but, as yet, we have said nothing about learning itself. Consequently, this chapter is devoted to providing a very full introduction to understanding learning. Significantly, there are a number of different ways of understanding this human process and a lot of misconceptions about it.

Theories of learning

Basically, there are four different theoretical approaches to learning:

- Behaviourist. Here the work of Pavlov, Skinner and Watson are well known. This has become a major way of looking at learning, partly because it focuses upon behavioural change. This is important for staff developers, but as a theoretical explanation of human learning it is profoundly flawed.
- Cognitive. The work of Piaget, Vygotsky and others fall into this category, and they are not perhaps so relevant for the work of staff developers and so they will be mentioned but briefly.
- Social learning. This is a later approach to learning and the work of Bandura and others will be discussed. Imitation of behaviour will be discussed here and the idea of modelling in general. This is an important approach for staff developers and we will spend a little more time looking at this.
- Experiential learning. This approach underlies all human learning and is fundamental to understanding the human process. We will concentrate upon this, examining Kolb's well-known but over-simple learning cycle, but Jarvis's own research will form a major part of this chapter in which he examines the complexity of the human learning process.

Definition of learning

There have been a number of different definitions, often relating to one of the four approaches mentioned above. Consequently, the behaviourist definition about learning being a change in behaviour as a result of experience has become as well known as the behaviourist theory. As we have already indicated, the theory is weak and so, therefore, is the definition. We would like to introduce a definition that falls into the final category, experiential learning, but covers all of the other categories:

> *Learning is the process of constructing and transforming experience into knowledge, skills, attitudes, values, emotions, senses, and beliefs.*

It can be seen here that all learning begins with our own understanding of our experiences in all situations and as we have these experiences we internalize them and acquire new knowledge, different skills, changed attitudes, different values, new emotional orientations, etc. However, these need not be totally new or changed – they can also be reinforcements of the knowledge, skill, etc that we have already.

Once we recognize that all experiences form the basis of learning, we can see how important it is for managers, and for staff developers, to be aware of the whole environment within which staff work. The organizational ethos has to be one which is good for learning and makes the staff feel good – satisfaction, if you like. This is what the learning organization should be like – all work experiences should be seen as opportunities for useful learning.

Understanding the learning process

Briefly, we will examine the first three approaches mentioned above – but we will spend a lot more time on the final one – because it actually includes the other three.

Behaviourism

Behaviourism, when applied to learning, involves stimulus and response and there are a number of famous theorists in this tradition:

- Most people are aware of the work of Pavlov (1927), whose research with dogs demonstrated that they can be taught to salivate at the sound of a bell, that is, that animals can be taught to respond to stimuli – classical conditioning.
- Thorndike *et al.* (1928) also showed that repetition of response to the stimuli will strengthen it.

- In addition, Skinner's (1974) work demonstrated that if the response is followed by a rewarding stimulus, it will also strengthen the response.

These approaches have been used in many forms of training, and they undeniably work with human beings as well as animals. However, they are criticized in human learning studies since they concentrate only on behaviour and make no reference to the cognitive processes and they are more concerned with teaching, or facilitating types of learning, than learning itself.

Cognitive approaches

Two such approaches will be mentioned here. Cognitive approaches to learning have been linked to the work of Piaget who was concerned to demonstrate that children's ability to conceptualize developed as they grew older. Unfortunately, he did not proceed with his studies into adulthood, but a few scholars have pursued them a little. A number of studies have, however, followed this up: showing that the questioning ability increases with ageing (Arlin, 1975), that adults became more reflective thinkers (Neugarten, 1977; Moshman, 1979), and the development of dialogic thought (Riegel, 1975). In different ways, all of these have been built into some later theoretical approaches to learning, especially in Argyris' and Schon's single- and double-loop learning. However, they have not always been built into models of training and learning – since bureaucratic-type organizations encourage non-reflective learning.

Another cognitive theorist is Gagne (Gagne *et al.*, 1992), who suggests that there are nine processes in learning:

- reception of stimuli by receptors
- registration of information by sensory registers
- selective perception for storage in the short-term memory
- rehearsal to maintain information in the short-term memory
- semantic encoding for storage in the long-term memory
- retrieval from the long-term memory to the working memory
- response generation to receptors
- performance in the learner's environment
- control of processes through executive strategies.

Gagne *et al.* demonstrate how instruction can be designed to follow this process of information transfer.

In Gagne's earlier work (1985), he concentrated on the conditions of learning which is something Jarvis (1995) discusses with reference to adults. These may be summarized as shown:

- learning is a basic human need
- learning is especially motivated when there is disharmony between an individual's perception and her or his perception of the world
- adult learners like to participate in the learning process
- adult learners bring their own experiences and meaning systems to the learning situation
- adult learners bring their own needs to the learning situation
- adult learners bring to the learning situation their own self-confidence, self-perception and self-esteem
- adults learn best when the self is not under threat
- adult learners need to feel that they are treated as adults
- adult learners have developed their own learning styles
- adult learners may learn at different speeds
- adults have developed a crystallized intelligence
- adults bring different physiological conditions to the learning situation.

Social learning theory

This is a quite fundamental approach to learning, since it merely incorporates all the other theories that we have discussed so far and goes on to show that people can learn by observing the actions of others and the outcomes of those actions without the help of a teacher or trainer.

Imitation is clearly the most common form of social learning, but it is deciding who should be role models that becomes more important. Clearly, this is important for staff developers who are involved in placements of new recruits and trainees. Knowing who are the experts who should become the role models should be part of the staff developer's job. It is also important when a company introduces mentoring schemes to know which members of staff should be trained as mentors.

Experiential learning

All learning begins with experience, so that this approach to learning is both the most fundamental and the most all-embracing. In fact, it incorporates all the previous ones. There are many well-known studies of experiential learning (see the references for a selection), but perhaps the most well-known is Kolb's learning cycle (see Figure 6.1).

Kolb (1984) claimed that learning could begin with a concrete experience and process through the four stages of his cycle:

- concrete experience
- reflective observation
- abstract conceptualization
- active experimentation.

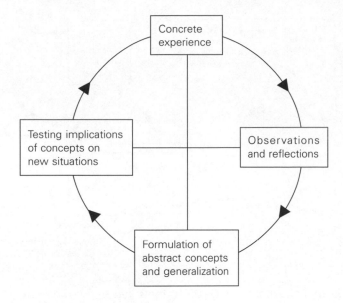

Figure 6.1 *Kolb and Fry's learning cycle (1975)*

However, Kolb was careful to point out that it is possible to start with the abstract conceptualization and move around the cycle to experimentation, experience and reflection. This cycle is beguilingly simple and has, therefore, become the basis of much thinking and planning about learning. Indeed, it has become almost the most well-known diagram to describe how human beings learn and it does incorporate much early theorizing – but later research shows that it is actually too simple.

Jarvis (1987, 1992, 1995) used Kolb as a starting point for his research into learning and while it is not the purpose of this chapter to describe this work in detail, Figure 6.2 illustrates his findings, although they are still far too simple. Since this research was undertaken, there have been further developments from it which lie beyond the scope of this book, but, significantly, when it was used in seminars with staff developers, its validity was recognized.

There are many routes through this diagram shown in Figure 6.2, but for the purposes of this book, there are three basic responses to experience and a number of different forms of learning:

- non-learning
- non-reflective learning
- reflective learning.

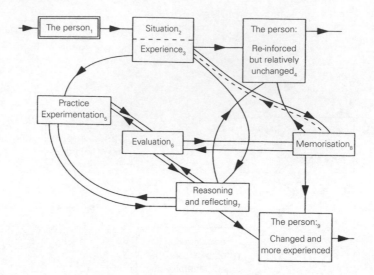

Figure 6.2   *Jarvis's elaboration of Kolb's learning cycle*

The routes through the diagram merely indicate some of the many ways in which human beings learn, and these are by no means exhaustive. Indeed, since individuals learn in both the skills and the cognitive domain at the same time, it is possible for these processes to be simultaneous. Human learning is a very complex process.

Non-learning

There are a variety of reasons why people do not learn from their experience:

- *Presumption* (1–2–3–4). They can presume about their situation and act almost unthinkingly. There is a sense in which this is what the experts do – they presume that they understand the situation and they then almost instinctively know what to do because they have learned it so thoroughly in the past. This is why experts might be conservative – they know that they know what to do and since it works for them, then they need a lot of convincing to change their ways. Their expertise may be such, that they actually do not need to learn!
- *Non-consideration* (1–2–3–4). People know that they are in a situation where they need to learn, but for a variety of reasons, they do not. They may be too busy, or too stressed, or they know it is easier to continue to do what they are already doing because that fits into the procedures of the company, the department or the unit, etc.

- *Rejection* (1–2–3–7–4 or 1–2–3–8–4). Individuals just reject the opportunity to learn for whatever reason. There may be a mental blockage, or the information that they have or the skills that they use may protect their own identity, etc in some way.

Non-reflective learning

Once again, three different types of learning are found:

- *Preconscious:* (1–2–3–6–4). Individuals have experiences which they remember but which never really enter into their consciousness. It usually takes a trigger to bring that experience to mind. We do this all the time, and are only aware when something brings it to our conscious memory.
- *Skills:* (1–2–3–5–6–4 or 1–2–3–5–6–9). This is basic training, drill or coaching. Individuals are helped to acquire and perform basic skills without necessarily understanding what they do or why they do it. It is not a very advanced form of learning but reflects some of the basic behaviourist ideas.
- *Memorization:* (1–2–3–6–4 or 1–2–3–6–9). Basically, we remember information without questioning it. Often this is what people regard as learning – merely internalizing the information that they have been taught. Again, it reflects basic behaviourist-type presuppositions.

Reflective learning

One of the things that those cognitivist theorists who went beyond Piaget noted was that adults tend to have more reflective approaches to their development – although this is not to deny that children are also reflective on occasions! Once again, there are three basic types of reflective learning:

- *Contemplation:* (1–2–3–7–9). This is a form of learning based upon pure thought. The learner starts from a basic premise and builds up an argument although never seeks to try it out in practice. Indeed, it might be impossible to do so – pure mathematics, philosophy, theology, etc are all academic disciplines that fall into this category, but so does a lot of our everyday thinking.
- *Reflective skills:* (1–2–3–5–7–5–8–6–9 or 1–2–3–7–5–8–6–9). Individuals reflect upon their skills or their role performance and for one reason or another they feel that they have to adjust their behaviour to account for a new situation. Having thought about it, they then produce new skills, role performance, etc. Now the significant thing about this is that this might come as a result of imitation of an expert, dissatisfaction with their own performance or because they have been taught to do things differently. They think about it – and then they do something about it. They own their own skills.

- *Experimental knowledge:* (l–2–3–7–5–7–8–9 or 1–2–3–5–7–8–9). For a variety of reasons, individuals reflect upon what they know and learn new knowledge – this is their own personal knowledge.

The final three forms of reflective learning do not mean that the learners have to acquire new knowledge, skills, attitudes, etc – they can actually agree with the status quo. However, as a result of the reflection they have made the knowledge and skills their own.

It will also be recognized that all the previous theories are contained in these different types of learning. A fundamental argument of this book is that the more staff developers understand these complex processes of learning, instead of trying to over-simplify them, the better will be the training programmes that they design. We will refer back to these during the remainder of this book.

At the same time it has to be recognized that, since learning begins with experience, all the experiences of work provide learning opportunities and once organizations accept this, then they can adapt their structures to become more flexible as they seek to learn from their employees' learning, etc.

Note that once this complex set of processes is recognized, it has a number of immediate repercussions for the job of the staff developer. The following brief sections outline a few of these.

Characteristics of adult learners

Learning is about people rather than processes – it is, therefore, about their own personal development throughout their lives, and the fact that all people learn from the cradle to the grave – but clearly their physical accuities, eg sight and hearing, will affect the way that they process their experiences.

Since learning is a lifelong process then age plays a less important part than was previously thought. Some of the large companies have shown this, as the Employers' Forum on Ageing is demonstrating. A great deal of research has been conducted on this as Worsley's (1993) study of age and employment has shown. Also see Jarvis, Dubelaar and Joyce's (1999) research on eldermentoring.

Motivation to learn

Staff developers act as motivators, when necessary. If people are out of harmony with their environment, they are usually motivated to want to learn so that they can rediscover a state of equilibrium. However, some employees may be unaware of their need, or be unwilling, to learn and in these instances staff developers have an important role to play since they have to help the employees move from non-consideration and rejection to a state of being prepared to learn from their experiences.

Understanding motivation is clearly part of the role of staff developers. Perhaps Maslow's (1954) hierarchy of needs is the most well-known approach to needs analysis. He suggested that there is a hierarchy from physiological to psychological, and while it might be over-simple, it is worth reproducing here:

- physiological needs, eg food, warmth
- safety needs, eg freedom from threat
- social needs, eg friendship
- esteem needs, eg respect from others, self-respect
- self-actualization, eg self-fulfilment.

It is significant that the higher order needs do not necessarily include financial reward! However, Herzberg *et al.* (1959) have postulated that there are two sets of work motivators which are similar in some ways to Maslow's hierarchy of needs without making them into a hierarchy:

- extrinsic factors, eg pay and working environment stem mainly from the external, organizational environment
- intrinsic factors are internal to the individuals and include advancement, recognition by others, etc.

Hence, staff developers should become motivators, using a variety of techniques to do so but it is best if this can be done without ever being in a situation of having to coerce employees to learn.

Learning strategies and learning styles

Not everybody learns in the same way, or indeed prefers to learn in the same way. That will be clear from the variety of types of learning that we have already discussed. Staff developers will find a number of different preferences, and they are described in the literature in a number of different ways. The following list was culled from a variety of different sources and the different types overlap. They are provided in order to enable staff developers to be aware of the different terminology and this list is an adaptation from Jarvis (1995).

- *Active versus passive.* Some people go out of their way to seek information and are self-directed while others await information being provided for them.

- *Assimilators versus accommodators.* Kolb suggests that assimilators are people who prefer thinking in abstract terms while accommodators prefer active experimentation.
- *Concrete versus abstract.* Concrete thinkers prefer to start with a concrete situation or experience while abstract thinkers prefer to start with the theoretical propositions.
- *Converger versus diverger.* Convergers are best at abstract thought and experimentation while divergers tend to reflect on concrete experience in a lateral manner.
- *Field dependent versus field independent.* Some people have to contextualize the whole and locate their experience within it while others think independently of the field – as discrete experiences.
- *Focusing versus scanning.* In problem-solving, focusers will examine the totality of the situation, generate hypotheses and modify them in the light of new information, while scanners will scan the problem, alight on a possible solution and operate as if it is the correct one until experience proves otherwise when they recommence the operation.
- *Holistic versus serialistic.* Some thinkers see phenomena as a whole, while others string the parts together.
- *Reflective versus impulsive.* Some thinkers reflect upon the whole while others impulsively select a possible solution and act upon it.
- *Rigidity versus flexibility.* Some people are fairly rigid in their approach to learning – once they have discovered a successful approach they prefer to keep to it, while others are quite flexible in their strategies.

Among the ways of testing the preferred learning styles of employees, two are well known: Kolb's learning style inventory which is based upon his learning cycle. Since Kolb's learning cycle is rather simple, his learning style inventory suffers the same basic weakness, although it is frequently used. Honey and Mumford (1986) consider that there are four basic types of people with different learning styles:

- *Activists* are gregarious people who are open-minded and enthusiastic about new things. They often approach problems by brainstorming. Usually they will try anything once and thrive on the challenge.
- *Reflectors* are cautious people who think about their experiences from a number of different perspectives over a relatively long period of time. They prefer to say little in meetings and discussions and are good at listening to others.
- *Pragmatists* tend to be down-to-earth, confident people who act quickly to try out new ideas and like to experiment with them. They like making practical decisions and look for better ways of doing things.

- *Theorists* are usually perfectionists who feel that ideas must fit into a rational scheme often linked to philosophy or basic principles. They think problems through in a step-by-step logical way. They tend to reject anything which doesn't fit into their 'mental set'.

The learning styles of Honey and Mumford are now being taken into account quite frequently and it is useful to read accounts of their approach to learning.

Transfer of learning or theory and practice?

Until very recently it was the received wisdom to talk about the application of theory to practice. However, if we look back at the learning diagrams (Figures 6.1 and 6.2), we can see that all learning begins with experience – and the immediate conclusion that we have to draw from this is that the workplace is as much a learning site as the classroom. The other conclusion to draw from the diagrams is that the people who learn allow their learning to affect their life, so that having learned in one situation they bring more experience to use in their learning to another. Consequently, people do not apply theory to practice – they use their theory in learning how to practise and, alternatively, they use their practical knowledge when they return to the classroom for their continuing education. (See Jarvis, 1999.)

It is important to note that there is no logical connection between knowing how to do something and being able to do it. You may be able to ride a bicycle but might be hard pressed to explain how you ride it! We have to understand in running training courses precisely what we want employees to learn, and how and where we want them to learn it.

It is important, therefore, that staff who are taught how to perform a skill or procedure be given an opportunity to learn to perform the skill or procedure in the actual work situation. In the same way, people who learn in the workplace how to perform a skill or procedure might be better performers if they learn the knowledge about the skill, eg:

- knowledge how a procedure should be performed
- knowledge that when a procedure is performed there are likely outcomes, and that there might be alternative strategies
- knowledge when to perform a skill or procedure
- knowledge why that skill or procedure should be performed.

These forms of knowledge relate to the different learning styles and strategies mentioned above, and by providing the whole picture, all employees will have their preferences met.

Work-based learning

It will be seen that one of the major arguments of this chapter is that learning takes place everywhere, especially in the workplace. Therefore, the staff developer has to ensure that the conditions are right for the organization to develop into a learning organization. It follows from the above that:

- the conditions for learning in the workplace should be as good as those in the training establishment
- there should be a consistent philosophy towards teaching, training and learning throughout the organization
- there should be mentors in the workplace, especially prepared to help employees learn to perform the skills and procedures that they have learned in their training
- opportunities to practise new skills and knowledge should be provided so that employees can build on their learning and transfer it from short-term to long-term memory through repetition, etc
- information should always be presented in a meaningful way, in the context of the whole operation
- assistance and feedback should be part of the whole philosophy of training throughout the entire organization.

Learning for personal and professional development

It may be seen from the learning diagram that all learning is biographical – everything we learn affects us. Even our non-learning can affect us. There is no separation in our learning between personal and professional learning – it is all personal. This has considerable implications for the work of the staff developer. Some companies have recognized this in some way and have tried to encourage staff to be involved in learning beyond the immediate scope of their work. Sometimes staff developers do have small budgets to assist employees in this way, and they should always endeavour to ensure that the relationship between personal and professional learning is fully recognized in the policies of the organization.

Staff developers should:

- fully understand the ways that people learn

- understand why some people do not want to learn and try to help them overcome their barriers to learning

- recognize that people learn by different styles and strategies

- establish mechanisms where every element of work is recognized as a potential learning situation

- have strategies in place, such as mentoring, to help all employees develop their learning in all situations

- recognize that all learning is personal development and assist in creating a work-based philosophy that allows for personal growth

- try to encourage and assist staff to learn beyond their immediate professional concerns

- co-operate with the personnel and welfare departments to ensure that there is a consistent strategy for personal growth and development of all employees.

References and Further Reading

Argyris, C (1982) *Reasoning, Learning and Action: Individual and Organisational,* Jossey-Bass, San Francisco.

Argyris, C and Schon, DA (1974) *Theory in Practice: Increasing Professional Effectiveness,* Jossey-Bass, San Francisco.

Argyris, C and Schon, DA (1978) *Organizational Learning: A Theory of Action Perspective,* San Francisco, Jossey-Bass.

Arlin, P (1975) Cognitive development in adulthood: a fifth stage?, *Developmental Psychology,* 11(5): 602–6.

Bandura, A (1977) *Social Learning Theory,* Prentice-Hall, Englewood Cliffs, NJ.

Corder, C (1990) *Teaching Hard, Teaching Soft,* Gower, Aldershot.

Gagne, RM (1985) *The Conditions of Learning: and Theory of Instruction,* (4th edn), Holt, Rhinehart and Winston, New York.

Gagne, RM, Briggs, LJ and Wager, W (1992) *Principles of Instructional Design,* Harcourt, Brace, Jovanovitch, Fort Worth.

Herzberg, R, Mausner, B and Snyderman, B (1959) *The Motivation to Work,* (2nd edn), John Wiley, New York.

Honey, P and Mumford, A (1986) *Manual of Learning Styles,* Peter Honey, Maidenhead.

Houle, CO (1980) *Continuing Learning in the Professions,* Jossey-Bass, San Francisco.

Jarvis, P (1987) *Adult Learning in the Social Context,* Croom Helm, London.

Jarvis, P (1992) *Paradoxes of Learning: On Becoming an Individual in Society*, Jossey-Bass, San Francisco.

Jarvis, P (1995) *Adult and Continuing Education: Theory and Practice*, (2nd edn), Routledge, London.

Jarvis, P (1999) *The Practitioner-Researcher: Developing Theory from Practice*, Jossey-Bass, San Francisco.

Jarvis, P, Dubelaar, J and Joyce, C (1999) *The Elder Mentor*, School of Educational Studies, University of Surrey, Guildford.

Kolb, DA (1984) *Experiential Learning: Experience as the source of Learning and Development*, Prentice-Hall, Englewood Cliffs, NJ.

Kolb, DA and Fry, R (1975) Towards an applied theory of experiential learning, in Cooper, CL (ed.), *Theories of Group Processes*, John Wiley and Sons, London.

Marsick, VJ (1987) *Learning in the Workplace*, Croom Helm, London.

Marsick, VJ (1990) Action learning and reflection in the workplace, in Mezirow, JD (ed.), *Developing Critical Self-reflection: Tools for Transformative Learning*, Jossey-Bass, San Francisco, pp.23–40.

Marsick, VJ and Watkins, K. (1990) *Informal and Incidental Learning in the Workplace*, Routledge, London.

Maslow, A (1954) *Motivation and Personality*, Harper and Row, New York.

Moshman, D (1979) To really get ahead, get a metatheory, in Kuhn, D (ed.), *Intellectual Development Beyond Childhood*, Jossey-Bass, San Francisco.

Neugarten, BL (1977) Adult personality: towards a psychology of the life-cycle, in Allman, JF and Jaffe, DT (eds), *Readings in Adult Psycholology: Contemporary Perspectives*, Harper, New York.

Pavlov, IF (1927) *Conditioned Reflexes: An Investigation of the Physiological Activity of the Cerebral Cortex*, (translated and edited by GV Anrep), Oxford University Press, London.

Piaget, J (1977) *The Essential Piaget*, (ed. HE Gruber and JJ Vonéche), Routledge and Kegan Paul, London.

Riegel, K (ed.) (1975) The development of dialetical operations, *Human Development*, 18: 1–238.

Skinner, BF (1974) *About Behaviorism*, Jonathan Cape, London.

Thorndike, EL, Bregman, EO, Warren, J, Tilton, JW and Woodyard, E (1928) *Adult Learning*, Macmillan, New York.

Watson, JB (1930) *Behaviorism*, Norton, New York.

Worsley, R (1993) *Life, Work and Livelihood in the Third Age*, Carnegie, Dunfermline. (Final report, Carnegie Inquiry into the Third Age.)

PART 2

The roles of human resource (HR) developers

Chapter 7

The roles of the staff developer

A staff developer's job can be very enjoyable but it requires leadership skills as well as a great deal of energy, patience, resourcefulness, initiative, efficiency and resilience. Staff developers bring their own values, understanding, attitudes and knowledge to their jobs and they often have a relatively free hand in making staff development decisions. They have to be good leaders, be able to delegate and have a good knowledge of how to motivate staff to participate in training activities.

In this chapter we try to provide a general outline of some of the roles and tasks of staff developers in relation to a systematic training cycle shown in Figure 7.1.

The cycle of training

The model shown in Figure 7.1 involves:

- identifying training needs
- planning and designing training
- delivering and presenting training
- evaluating the training programme.

Various research undertakings have shown that there are at least 20 different roles which may be undertaken in the context of a training model, ranging from a needs analyst, programme designer, instructor and administrator to an evaluator and statistician. At times, staff developers also have to act as counsellors or career advisors. In this chapter, and in the following ones, we outline the various roles and give examples of the tasks undertaken by staff developers. The practicalities of undertaking the various roles are outlined in detail in Part 3.

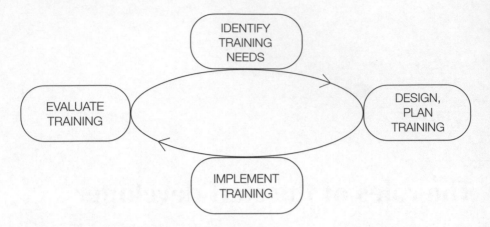

Figure 7.1   *A systematic training model*

Source: EOSCNTO (DfEE) Crown copyright is reproduced with the permission of the controller of Her Majesty's Stationery Office.

The multifaceted role

The duties of a staff developer are extremely varied; if asked to explain precisely what they do, they would be hard pressed to summarize them. We have given a list of the main roles below. There are also many more subroles, which have been described by McLagan (1983) and Hargreaves (1995):

- strategist
- task and needs analyst
- manager of training and development
- programme designer
- instructional writer
- media specialist for audio-visual material
- programme administrator
- facilitator
- instructor
- trainer
- statistician
- transfer agent
- evaluator
- assessor for NVQs
- communicator
- individual development counsellor

- theoretician
- self-developer
- consultant
- marketer.

There are many tasks which may be undertaken within each role as discussed by Pinto and Walker (1978), McLagan (1983) and Hargreaves (1995). For example, in the role of needs analyst there are at least five major tasks and many minor ones. The American Society for Training and Development report (McLagan, 1983) listed over 100 'critical outputs' for the roles listed. For example, these 'outputs' describe an end-product such as a report produced by the evaluator. Although we describe most roles and many tasks in this book it is impossible for us to discuss every eventuality, so we have tended to concentrate on the major roles and on some of the tasks which are most often performed. In the next few chapters (8–10) we shall look more fully into the theoretical aspects of each of the key roles. We discuss them broadly in the sequence in which they occur within a training cycle:

- starting with planning and defining training needs (strategist, needs analyst)
- looking for ways to match needs to the supply of relevant training initiatives (manager of training and development)
- actually running some events (trainer)
- designing in-house programmes where necessary (programme designer)
- evaluating the events (evaluator).

Of course, others are support roles such as marketer, administrator, etc. In Chapters 12 to 15 (Part 3), we discuss some of the practicalities involved in working as staff developer, eg some major tasks involved in designing programmes and presenting training events.

Hargreaves has actually analysed her own role as a staff developer in a science research organization in Britain (Hargreaves, 1995). In Figure 7.2 we show the time she spent on eight key roles while staff developer.

Some 28 per cent of her time was spent in managing the training function, eg planning and implementing programmes, matching training needs with supply, obtaining resources. Some 25 per cent was spent as programme administrator, ie getting all participants, trainers, and resources together and ensuring the smooth running of each training initiative.

As far back as 1978, Pinto and Walker pointed out that the training and development profession was in flux and that it was sometimes difficult to determine precisely what training professionals did in the course of their work. The situation has not changed very much! This is partly because of the rapidly changing situation within which we work, because management is aware that so much needs to be done and because professionals are also creating their own roles and specialisms. Indeed, the HRD specialist is playing a key role in

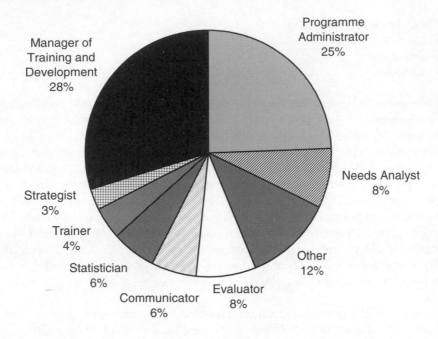

Figure 7.2 *Approximate percentage of time spent carrying out various roles by a staff developer in a research organization*
Source: Hargreaves, (1995)

various aspects of personnel development at work. Furthermore, the current high incidence of job restructuring or short-term contract jobs in many countries has meant that some staff developers are being called upon to train new staff, or to counsel for career change or early retirement. Development of advanced technology, including computing programming applications such as the Internet, has meant that many people have to update to the new technology and to ways of obtaining information or using equipment. Thus, it seems unrealistic to expect the competencies of such a rapidly expanding profession to remain unchanged. We can expect them to continue to change very rapidly for the next few years.

We would emphasize that the overview presented here is not what staff developers have to do, it is just to illustrate some of the different things that they might choose to do, or are expected to do at work! Indeed, it would be astonishing if individual staff developers had the time or the expertise to undertake all of the activities described here and in Part 3.

Matching training needs to supply

In Figure 7.1 we showed that, basically, there are four main stages in a training model:

- finding out what the training needs are (for instance, do secretaries need to update their skills?, how good is the quality of products?, are health and safety seminars required?)
- planning a way to meet those needs, (eg buying in a course to be run in-house, sending people to the local college for training or designing a programme to be run in-house
- presenting a training event (or organizing another professional to act as trainer or presenter or instructor)
- getting some feedback to see if a training event was successful in terms of what staff learned and if they could use their new skills at work.

There are many different aspects to a deceptively simple problem of identifying training needs and matching them to a supply of training. These include:

- planning a strategy
- specifying the standards required
- assessing the numbers of staff involved
- how, where and when the training curriculum should be implemented
- resources needed (including funds which from time to time will need to be negotiated with line managers or the management team)
- planning a timetable of training events
- putting the training into operation
- deciding on the evaluation strategy.

Precise job titles and job specifications are likely to provide some idea of the duties that organizations expect their staff developers to undertake. Before deciding on the roles and tasks, it is advisable to discuss the HRD specialist's area of responsibility with the directors, management team or the training manager in the organization. For example, in some large organizations, there may be several staff in a training department, each with a variety of specialisms and areas of responsibility. Some staff developers or line managers may be responsible for computer training, while others may organize management training. In smaller companies, however, a single staff developer may work only part time and perform only a few staff development activities each day while coping with other work, such as personnel management. In some organizations, line managers take over much of the responsibility of organizing vocational training while the staff developer organizes all other staff development activities, eg health and safety courses, first aid courses and management development.

The qualifications of the staff developer will also have some bearing on the extent of their responsibilities. For instance, it would be inappropriate to counsel staff in the workplace if this were not expected or if they had not acquired appropriate qualifications. In this instance, another qualified specialist may already have been employed to perform that function.

In the next chapters, we look at some of the roles in detail.

Staff developers should:

- be prepared to undertake a variety of roles

- remain aware that the roles may change depending on the needs of staff and employers

- always try to match training needs to relevant supply

- prioritize their roles.

References and Further Reading

Hargreaves, PM (1995) *The Training Officer: A Cost-effective Role in a Science Research Organisation?*, unpublished PhD thesis, University of Surrey.

London, M (1988) *Change Agents: New Roles and Innovation Strategies for Human Resource Professionals*, Jossey-Bass, San Francisco.

McLagan, P (1983) *Models for Excellence: The Conclusions and Recommendations of the ASTD Training and Development Competency Study*, American Society for Training and Development Press, Washington, DC.

McLagan, P (1989) *Models for HRD Practice*, American Society for Training and Development Press, Alexandria, VA.

Pace, RW, Smith, PC and Mills, GE (1991) *Human Resource Development: The Field*, Prentice-Hall, Englewood Cliffs, NJ.

Pepper, AD (1984) *Managing the Training and Development Function*, Gower, Aldershot.

Pettigrew, AM, Jones, GR and Reason, PW (1982) *Training and Development Roles in their Organisational Setting*, Manpower Services Commission Training Division, Sheffield.

Pinto, PR and Walker, JW (1978) *A Study of Professional Training and Developmental Roles and Competences*, American Society for Training and Development Press, Baltimore, MD.

Pinto, PR and Walker, JW (1982) What do training and development professionals really do?, *Training and Development Journal*, 28: 58–64.

Chapter 8

Roles of strategist, needs analyst, manager of training and development and marketer

In the previous chapter we discussed the numerous roles enacted by staff developers and their ability to cope with the complexity of their work. We have linked some of the roles in the sequence in which they are likely to occur within the Training Cycle in Figure 8.1. For example, the role of strategist or planner is at the beginning of the cycle, while evaluator and statistician are towards the end.

In this chapter we concentrate on roles which are undertaken prior to the implementation of training, ie adopting a strategy, analysing training needs, attempting to match training needs with supply, marketing events and ensuring that organization and administration are correct down to the last detail. In the next chapter we discuss the further 'support' or 'behind the scene' roles of programme designer and instructional writer which are undertaken prior to implementing a programme. Roles involved in actual delivery of training events, such as teaching or instructing or coaching are also discussed in Chapter 9.

Strategist

Strategists work closely with the management team in putting forward ideas and discussing future plans, eg the needs of the organization, teams of staff or departments are periodically discussed when deciding on the future strategy for staff development. Adopting a training strategy is often a joint effort between the management team and staff developers. It is impossible for them

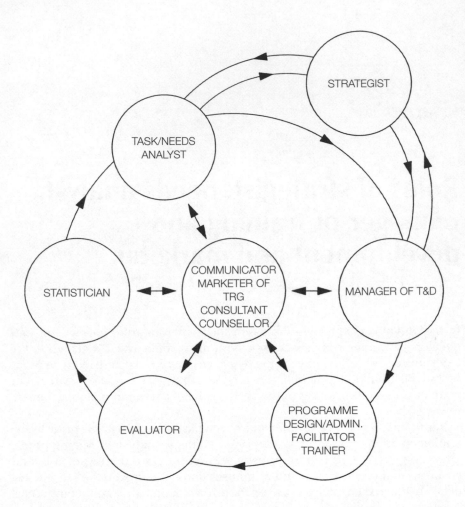

Figure 8.1 *Some key roles of the human resource developer linked to the training cycle*

Note: The roles shown in the centre of the model are those which might be enacted at all stages of the training cycle.

to act independently in this role unless they have a seat on the management board or at least have regular meetings about staff development with senior management. On the other hand, in some organizations staff developers act solely on suggestions from directors, line managers and other staff who provide information on funds and time available for staff development.

Needs analyst

The needs analyst is concerned with defining organizational and staff needs in terms of skills and technological updating and health and safety initiatives. The job is also concerned with identifying gaps in performance, monitoring staff and management requests for education and training and determining priorities. There are, therefore, three main sources from which training needs arise:

Organizational needs

Being a member of the management team clearly helps staff developers to see some of the future training needs for the organization. Awareness of organizational needs arise from:

- an examination of an organization's internal systems, procedures and resources
- understanding its culture and ways of working
- health and safety initiatives
- the quality of products.

In large transnational and national organizations, reviews of this nature will already have been undertaken by management teams, since it is their responsibility and a complex and time-consuming task. However, in smaller companies, staff developers may be more involved in undertaking such analyses.

Usually there will be a need for technological updating in terms of software, hardware and manufacturing methods. There may also be various problems which have to be remedied, such as a lack of marketing expertise or unacceptably high sickness rates. Training specialists cannot hope to remedy all faults quickly and easily, but it is their role to discuss staff development initiatives with the management team and line managers in cases where perceived organizational training needs are involved. It will also be necessary to induct new recruits into the organization, as awareness of their needs is also very important.

In order to be able to analyse the needs of all staff, staff developers have to be knowledgeable about the organizations in which they work, knowing what skills are required and what needs employees perceive themselves as having.

Skills required for jobs or tasks

Line managers are a major source of information about this aspect of need, but staff developers may be asked by them either to undertake a specific task analysis, or arrange for this to be undertaken. This involves analysing the necessary competencies required for its performance. Generally, jobs or tasks may be analysed in terms of the skills, or behaviours, or attitudes necessary to complete them. A *skills analysis* describes the skills necessary to do a job or task. A *task analysis* describes what behaviours are required to complete a task efficiently. For example, a new production line may require the expertise of skilled operators. Although information may be available about the number of steps which may constitute a task, in some instances a line manager might express concern about how a person has performed a task in terms of process or output, and this is a *performance analysis*. A performance objective sets out the required performance standards expected of staff, and staff are then trained to achieve the necessary performance level.

To establish whether there is a gap in performance of a job or whether a refresher course or updating is necessary, line managers will have to be aware of an individual's efficiency in terms of output, quality of work and inter-personal effectiveness in working with others as a team. They usually inform staff developers of the changes required for each member of staff, both in terms of standards expected at the end of training courses and the time limitations within which the staff should work.

Individual needs

Individuals also have their own needs, which may be both work-related and leisure-related. Some more enlightened companies are concerned with leisure needs, as well as vocational ones. In respect to leisure-time interests, some companies, like Ford, have already introduced voucher schemes, whereby they help their employees to undertake interest education classes in their spare time. However, other companies have also organized courses for their employees both during work time, and outside of it. One City of London company, for instance, organizes French classes for its employees at 8 am one morning a week, and these conclude at 9.30, when it is time for the office to open. In this instance, the company also benefits since it has business in France. Nevertheless, all employees who wish to can attend the class, irrespective of whether their work requires them to use French. Staff developers may also be able to provide educational guidance to individuals, about where they can find the type of course that they would like to follow. If they know of staff who have training needs which, if met would benefit the organization, they should always ensure that those staff are informed when relevant courses are being organized.

Staff developers should collate the lists of needs and these form the basis on which the staff development programme can be prioritized and planned. Rarely are there sufficient funds for all the needs to be met, so that planning the programme is a tricky business – with each probable event being bud-geted. Indeed, it is very necessary to work out the minimum number of places filled that will make any event viable – filling places is important, both educationally and economically. If there are too many participants in an event, then the dynamics inhibit effective training and, if there are too few, it is not always economically viable.

Staff developers need to plan, co-ordinate and develop the whole of the staff development function, sometimes at least one or two years ahead. The planning must include work-based, 'at the desk or bench' initiatives. Although training and education can provide the skills and knowledge necessary for many work-related tasks, there is much that cannot be learned through formal education and training programmes. For example, engineers gain a great amount of experiential learning at the work-bench from colleagues, either formally or informally. Practicalities of undertaking a needs analysis are discussed in Chapter 12.

Manager of training and development

Once a provisional programme has been prepared then the managerial function of the staff developer comes to the fore. It is necessary to do the following:

- Decide how to match training needs with supply.
- Negotiate for resources.
- Finalize the staff development programme.
- Plan a timetable of training events.
- Recruit staff to teach, within the budget allowed for that event.
- Market the programme, so that it recruits the staff at which it is aimed.
- Prepare for the evaluation of each session, both immediately after the session has been conducted and at a later date to assess its impact on the work situation/workers.

This, then, is the role which is concerned with the smooth running of the training function as a whole, requiring a number of different skills.

Recruitment of trainers and instructors

It is rare for staff developers to possess expert knowledge about the many specialized topics covered by education and training programmes. For example, they may have the expertise to run courses in, say, 'time management' but may lack the skills to run courses on, 'advanced computer programming'. If courses are to be run in-house, it will almost certainly be necessary to build up a register of trainers who can be employed – both from within the company and external to it. It is, therefore, necessary to put into place procedures to recruit staff to run the training programme. Staff developers need to know the experts within the company who are keen to share their expertise with others, but they may still have to bring in outside experts to conduct much of the training.

Procedures for in-house recruitment might be fairly informal, in the first instance. For example, individuals who are known to possess expertise might be approached to see if they are interested, or staff developers can advertise around the organization, asking for interested people to contact them. It would be wise, from the outset, to devise an application form, asking them about their knowledge, qualifications and experience in the teaching or training of adults. There may be many members of staff who would share their expertise, but have no experience of teaching or training, and if this occurs, then it might be wise to seek training for them by contacting a local university or college of education or adult education institute.

However, it is often necessary to bring in outside consultants to cover the wide range of courses needed. Anybody can set themselves up as a training consultant, and so it is best to interview potential trainers, check their qualifications and track record before employing them. It is also necessary to recognize that those who charge the highest fees are not necessarily the best! Presentation plays a major role in consultants' marketing, and so be sure that those who are employed have both the knowledge and the proven skills to do what is required. It is very important to be specific in employing outsiders so that their expertise may be used to the best advantage of the company.

Staff developers should gradually build up their own bank of trainers whom they know and trust. This knowledge should come from the evaluations that training staff receive from participants in events. It is important to maintain contact with trusted trainers, so that they can help develop programmes in areas of their own expertise.

An alternative strategy, of course, is to send staff to local or more distant educational institutes for specialized training, eg engineering training. In practice, on-site and off-site courses are usually arranged, depending on the level of expertise available and the equipment needed.

Marketer of training and development

Many companies do not have a culture of continuous training and, indeed, for some the idea of training on-site, and having a training department, is something of a novelty – even an expensive luxury. Staff developers sometimes have to market their expertise and their programmes within the organization. Closely allied to the communication role, marketing staff development activities are often undertaken informally within the organization. However, other communication networks exist for publicising training, eg newsletters, e-mail, posters. Usually advertising results in places being filled and promotes cost-effectiveness. It is necessary to remember that if places are not filled, then it is not always because the staff are not interested – they may not know about it, or they may not be able to come. If there is interest, but staff cannot come, it is useful to find a mechanism whereby that interest can be recorded in the training department so that they may be invited to the next training event.

In the following chapter we discuss the roles of programme designer, instructional writer, trainer and programme administrator

---

Staff developers should:

- obtain the views of managers and staff when planning the programme or curriculum, or even better, involve them in the planning, so that they know that they can send their own staff

- be systematic in recording all the training needs they learn about, putting names against individual needs, etc. They should go back to the person, unit or department to discuss or provide information, especially if, as a result, a training event on the topic will be organized

- be careful and systematic in the way they go about recruiting part-time trainers. What goes on in the training session itself is more important than the way that consultants present their expertise. If necessary, sit in with new part-time trainers and make your own assessment of their expertise

- always inform the line management when employing outside consultants – and the finance office!

- make sure that the venue is acceptable and suitable. Ensure that it has all the resources and facilities that are required

- be prepared to share their own expertise with staff, talk to them about the successes and disappointments of past training events in terms of previous methods, venues, procedures, especially if a staff developer is new to an organization. Do not bore new colleagues. Never compare the present situation unfavourably with previous ones.

References and Further Reading

Boydell, TH (1990) *A Guide to the Identification of Training Needs*, London, Department of Education and Employment.

Corder, C (1990) *Teaching Hard, Teaching Soft*, Gower, Aldershot.

Field, L and Drysdale, D (1991) *Training for Competence*, Kogan Page, London.

Hackett, P (1981) *Interview Skills Training: Practice Packs for Trainers*, Institute of Personnel Management, London.

Jessup, G (1991) *Outcomes: NVQs and the Emerging Model of Education and Training*, Falmer, London.

Kenney, J and Reid, M (1986) *Training Interventions*, Institute of Personnel Management, London.

Laird, D (1978) *Approaches to Training and Development*, Addison-Wesley, Reading, Mass.

Pepper, AD (1984) *Managing the Training and Development Function* (2nd edn 1992), Gower, Aldershot.

Peterson, R (1992) *Training Needs Analysis in the Workplace*, Kogan Page, London.

Platt, J (1981) On interviewing one's peers, *British Journal of Sociology*, 32(1): 75–91.

Robinson, DG and Robinson, JC (1989) *Training for Impact: How to Link Training to Business Needs and Measure the Results*, Jossey-Bass, San Francisco.

Chapter 9

Roles of programme designer, instructional writer, facilitator, trainer and programme administrator

In this chapter we consider further roles that need to be undertaken particularly if staff developers are designing and implementing their own training initiatives with the intention of running them in-house. In many instances they arrange for staff to attend locally run courses or ask consultants to come in to run specific events. Even then it is important to consider the main aims and objectives of the training event, how long it should run and the sequence of activities. Sometimes specialist trainers or consultants are able to adapt courses to the particular requirements of an organization. It is important for the designer to take into account how adults learn and the best method for each individual.

Programme designer

In a work situation a staff developer may not intend learners to make major changes as a result of a series of learning events, but rather to reinforce or build on existing learning. For example, an organization's contracts department may offer a series of refresher courses to all staff involved in obtaining new contracts. The purpose of the workshops may be to remind line managers of their continuing need to be aware of legal or technical problems in taking out new contracts and abiding by the terms of existing ones. It is also important that the courses are relevant and the learning can be effectively transferred to the day-to-day work situation.

Sometimes organizations have a prescriptive programme design which is used for months or years. It is used when an organization requires specific standards and large numbers of people need to be trained, eg training programmes in customer care, marketing, sales, computing, accountancy. Here, elements of the training course are presented in a given sequence and it is difficult to alter the design until the model is updated. In other instances, staff developers are offered greater flexibility in planning and designing training programmes. In this instance, the staff developer may obtain input from a variety of sources, eg unions, management, resource-providers, fund-holders, directors, line managers, consultants, computer staff and, of course, the trainees themselves. This will help them to decide on learning or training objectives. It is essential to co-ordinate the whole process and negotiate aspects of funding, accommodation, time-scales, numbers of trainers, numbers of participants, standards required, training objectives and evaluation.

Instructional writer

Nearly always, staff developers have to write a synopsis of activities. Designing and writing materials for educational events is a very skilled job and often staff developers are expected to produce material with little or no training. Some of the work involves producing the following:

- distance learning materials
- advertising materials
- hand-outs
- booklets
- diagrams
- graphs
- tables.

It is clear that many of these skills require good personal computer skills and having good audio-visual aid facilities. Most written training material has to be very clear and concise. Audio-visual material and hand-outs are discussed further in Chapter 16

Facilitator

Facilitators often apply techniques for organizational development, sometimes helping people to learn in a group. For example, they may promote discussions between departments by organizing seminars. They may also promote action learning and reflection by individuals and the consequent exchange of the new information with colleagues. Although they sometimes work as trainers, staff developers also sometimes facilitate the learning behind the scenes. For example, they may negotiate for study leave on behalf of a student or work to help them gain some financial support, etc. In effect, *facilitation* of learning is a type of non-directive teaching. For instance, Rogers (1967) uses this term when 'discovery' learning or experiential learning is involved and the students control their learning and learning goals themselves.

We have to be careful when we use this word because many trainers restrict it to facilitation of learning in individual groups, seminars or workshops – rather than adopting the wider perspective that we have employed here. Indeed Rogers (1969) discusses the work of a facilitator. This includes:

- setting the initial mood or climate of the class or group
- making available a wide range of resources for learning, including field trips, equipment, etc
- acting as counsellor, lecturer or advisor.

The facilitator may also become part of a learning group – exchanging ideas and learning from other members and, although remaining as leader, accept his or her own limitations.

Trainers and instructors

Usually instructors assist with job training. For example, they are often involved in practical military training, teaching people to drive or to fly aeroplanes. They also present job-related theoretical knowledge. Indeed, in US literature, an instructor is a trainer and there is no difference. In fact the instructor may be a teacher of almost any form!

When acting as trainers, training professionals are expected to make lively and interesting presentations, also ensuring that participants are encouraged to make useful contributions to the proceedings. For example, they might lead seminars, workshops, courses, discussions, lectures, open forums, etc.

Instructors and trainers should be good communicators, always clear and precise and ensuring that they are fully understood. They should also convey sincerity and self-confidence by tone of voice and body language. Often they teach people of widely differing abilities and attitudes and so they also need a very supportive approach. However, because staff developers are dealing with a wide range of competent adults, they must take control of a teaching situation and learn to accept criticism and use it constructively. Basically, criticism is an opportunity to learn, not always in the most comfortable of situations but, nevertheless, teachers who fail to learn from others are not helping their own understanding of their role.

Not only should trainers learn from criticism, they do not know everything about every aspect of the organization in which they work, so that they should also be prepared to learn from colleagues. Colleagues may not wish to act as teachers themselves, but they will often share their learning with staff developers, so that the latter can act as intermediaries in the teaching process. However, colleagues who have the expertise but do not wish to act as trainers, may be prepared to share a session with the staff developer and this is a good way for everybody to learn. Staff developers may be able to lead that session on another occasion, or the expert colleague may be more prepared to do it on a subsequent occasion.

While acting as a trainer, it is important to promote the transfer of learning by reminding course participants of how they can apply the newly learned skills and knowledge to the work situation material. It is even better if the knowledge and skills are presented in a practical manner. In this context, they act as a transfer agent. Trainers usually try to take their students' preferred method of learning into account. Sometimes they apply new techniques to their teaching strategies to see if they are helpful to students. In effect, they are theoreticians – putting theory into practice.

Programme administrators

The role of programme administrator is extremely important, complex and time-consuming, it is concerned with the organizing of specific events and ensuring that they run smoothly. Organizing abilities are needed to ensure that participants, trainers, tutors and required learning materials are all available at a given location, date and time, supporting course participants where necessary. Negotiating skills are essential to obtain reductions in fees for hotel accommodation, etc or for the use of resources on a day-to-day basis. In the next chapter we shall discuss the roles of general administrator, evaluator, statistician, consultant and counsellor.

Staff developers should ensure that:

- they understand the intricacies of programme design

- they are good planners, taking everything into consideration before the event

- they understand that it does not matter how good the tutor or trainer, etc, if the organization of the event is bad, then the event itself will be bad

- they have contingency plans in case anything goes wrong

- the learning is of practical relevance.

References and Further Reading

Corder, C (1990) *Teaching Hard, Teaching Soft: A Structured Approach to Planning and Running Effective Training Courses*, Gower, Aldershot.

Guliano, D (1984) Instructing, in Nadler (ed.), *The Handbook of Human Resource Development*, John Wiley, New York, pp. 8.1–8.20.

Houle, CO (1972) *The Design of Education*, Jossey-Bass, San Francisco.

Jaques, D (1984) *Learning in Groups*, Croom Helm, London.

Jarvis, P (1995) *Adult and Continuing Education: Theory and Practice* (2nd edn), Routledge, London.

Kenney, J and Reid, M (1986) *Training Interventions*, Institute of Personnel Management, London.

McLagan, P (1983) *Models for Excellence: The Conclusions and Recommendations of the ASTD Training and Development Competency Study*, American Society for Training and Development Press, Washington, DC.

Rogers, C (1967) *The Facilitation of Significant Learning*, in Siegel, L (ed.), *Instruction: Some Contemporary Viewpoints*, Chandler Publishing Co, Pennsylvania.

Rogers, C (1969) *Freedom to Learn*, Merrill Publishing Co, Colombus Ohio.

Wiggs, GD (1984) Designing learning programs, in Nadler, L (ed.), *The Handbook of Human Resource Development*, John Wiley, New York.

Chapter 10

The administrator, evaluator, statistician, consultant and counsellor

In this chapter we consider other roles of staff developers that tend to involve administration, evaluation of the whole training function and giving advice. In many ways they are as important as actually providing face-to-face training because this information provides a rationale for investing in future training. Additionally, directors, the management team or other staff sometimes need up-to-date training-related information quickly. For example, staff developers may be called upon at a moment's notice to advise the most junior to the most senior staff in their organization about the education or training provision. Consequently, these five roles are linked together here since they reflect another approach to the staff developer's multifaceted role.

The administrator

In the process of defining and implementing, staff developers act as general administrators and accountants and monitor the total training process. There are a whole host of staff development activities undertaken within an organization that need to be documented in terms of location, dates, trainers or tutors, names of participants, costs, etc. Policy documents may be prepared and the core training curricula or programmes will need to be discussed with management, union representatives, etc. Linked to this is the requirement to monitor each individual's participation in on-site or off-site learning programmes in order to ensure that all staff are given as equal opportunities as possible for their continued development.

Budgets

Managing budgets and investigating cost-effectiveness are also important aspects of the work. Often the proposed programmes have to be prepared while the training budget for the year is still being negotiated. Moreover, once the budget is fixed for the year, the total costs of training initiatives have to fall within given targets.

Additionally, in most organizations staff developers have the responsibility for administering the training budget once it has been negotiated, either in total or in part. They may need to negotiate additional funds for setting up new or ongoing training facilities, which may include office accommodation, video and audio recording equipment, etc. Costs for in-house and external training initiatives should be documented in terms of capital outlay and ongoing costs. Sometimes most of the costs of education and training initiatives are shared between departments. This latter situation has drawbacks, especially at such times as the end of the financial year when money is scarce since the heads of some departments may not have the resources to allow their staff to participate in courses while other departments are more wealthy and their heads can release staff for training. Thus, education and training opportunities within the organization may be unevenly distributed and even create internal problems and jealousies.

Staff developers need to keep a full account of how their money is spent since it is often necessary to present accounts to management and, where appropriate, to sponsoring organizations at the end of each financial year or each project.

Records

It is also necessary for the staff developer to keep clear and concise records of staff development. This is emphasized for a number of reasons, not least because some courses may lead to certification, nationally, or even internationally, recognized qualifications and credit transfers of qualifications or access to new courses. Moreover, interest groups such as unions may need to be informed regularly about numbers of staff who have been given opportunities for education and training and at what level that training has occurred. Usually personal training records of staff are kept on file, either in a computer database or in personal training portfolios, usually one portfolio for each person. The relevant information from these can then be used by trainers when preparing and running training courses.

It is important to maintain a computerized database for all of these reasons. Staff developers need, therefore, a basic knowledge of computing and the ability to use a spread sheet. However, there might be a preference to use commercially available packages for such records. In some countries where data protection legislation exists, it is advisable to confer with your organization's personnel department so as to ensure that staff are given the right to see their personal training records on request.

Safety

Generally, the working environment has to be safe and staff developers should ensure that any visiting lecturers, tutors or trainers they employ should be aware of, and comply with health and safety regulations.

Evaluator

One very important role is that of evaluator. Staff developers and the management team need to have information on the success or otherwise of initiatives run by the training department. Information has to be gained about the extent to which the course or session met the objectives of the participants and the impact of each initiative on job performance. They also need information on which courses were run, for whom, and the cost-effectiveness of the training function, particularly in terms of the extent to which the new learning was transferred to the workplace.

Evaluation is generally a time-consuming exercise as training outcomes have to be discussed with line managers, sales or marketing staff and the participants in the various initiatives. There may be, however, a few problems about reporting back to line managers on training sessions since the participants might regard the staff developer as a 'spy' for the line manager, and thus they would not necessarily share all their other learning aspirations with the staff developer. Hence, the extent to which there is feedback has to be very carefully considered. In some instances, evaluation might entail becoming an assessor for National Vocational Qualifications. The practicalities of evaluating events are discussed in Chapter 17.

Statistician

One of the functions of staff developers is to maintain a full record for management of the amount of development and training that is conducted on an annual basis by the organization. This usually includes:

- number of courses completed
- number of courses undertaken off-site
- attendance at each course, highlighting the most successful
- courses that do not run because of lack of support
- individualized support given – number of consultations

- total number of hours of training taken up by staff
- costs of initiatives per department
- costs of training per member of staff
- number of significant or innovative training events organized
- academic qualifications or certificates gained by members of staff as a result of organizational training activities.

All of this information can be maintained on a database and communicated to all directors, managers and their staff on a regular basis. It is also the type of information that might be included in a newsletter produced by the training department for all members of staff. If the training department does not have its own newsletter, it might be wise for staff developers to ensure that they have a regular slot in the staff newsletter or newspaper to communicate these activities.

Consultant for managers and staff

Staff developers will, almost certainly, be expected to act as in-house training consultants. Frequently they are asked to advise management teams and line managers about training strategy for all staff, standards of courses and their content and many other training and development matters. Thus, they should know about all the training initiatives that have occurred in their organization, even those being run within individual departments. They should also keep abreast of new developments in education and training, both nationally and internationally. Only when the staff developer is knowledgeable, can senior management have confidence in the type of information and advice they are given to help them make informed policy decisions about training.

Another aspect of the consulting role of staff developers is problem-solving. Staff developers can be called into other departments to help with training-related problems, so that the ability to solve problems and to cope with pressures are essential attributes of the job. The extent to which this occurs, naturally, depends in part upon the level of trust and respect obtained by the staff developer in the organization concerned.

Indeed, the ability to maintain good interpersonal relationships is essential. A recent survey of staff developers working for a research council showed that good personal relationships were placed high on the list of attributes which they thought were needed (Hargreaves, 1995). Other attributes include being a good communicator, possessing good interpersonal skills and displaying flexibility. Those personal qualities are essentially those which permit individuals to adjust to the culture in which they find themselves and to respond to the problems with which they are presented.

Educational guidance and counselling

Staff developers are frequently asked for advice. This can take a number of different forms such as educational guidance, career guidance and personal counselling. As society is becoming more complex, there are a great number of opportunities for staff to further their education, both personally and professionally. Naturally, staff developers cannot be expected to know all the possibilities that exist but they usually build up a library of relevant prospectuses and brochures, so that staff can consult them. These may vary from the local prospectuses from the adult education institute, the college of further education and university to professional associations and organizations offering courses and lectures.

Career counselling, however, is a little more specialized and staff developers have to be aware of the pitfalls in embarking upon this, especially if some of it is undertaken as a matter of course during annual appraisal meetings with line managers. Additionally, staff developers might be approached to offer more personal counselling. If sufficiently qualified, they might take on this role, but they should recognize that counselling about work cannot be divorced from counselling about self (see Woolfe *et al.* 1987) and this might not be simply a matter of giving advice on the basis of 'if I were you'. Much of this type of work is concerned with individuals who experience problems at work such as stress, or poor interpersonal relationships. Individuals should be helped to think out their own solutions to problems. As Woolfe *et al.* (1987) point out, work-related counselling tasks should be undertaken within a framework of empathy. Sometimes joint discussions between line managers, the individuals themselves and staff developers, possibly with suggestions of appropriate training initiatives, may help to solve a problem.

Marital or health problems may also affect the work-related performance of an individual and, in the case of serious problems, staff developers should advise individuals to consult welfare officers or regional health or social services rather than try to act as counsellors themselves. Remember, counselling is a skilled undertaking and if unskilled people get themselves involved they can actually make matters worse, so that it is wiser to refer the individual to the specialists.

In Part 2 we have discussed some of the major roles of staff developers. There are also other roles such as leader, communicator and also the emerging role as assessor for National Vocational Qualifications. In the next chapter we focus on various aspects of managing a wide range of tasks and roles. In Part 3 we shall discuss some of the day-to-day practicalities of implementing the training cycle.

Staff developers should:

- ensure that there are up-to-date books, brochures and advice magazines available in the training department

- always be supportive of staff who come to them with a problem

- remain aware of the boundaries of their role

- intervene in workplace situations only after consideration of the ethical issues involved and, where appropriate, in conjunction with colleagues

- keep a register of experts and refer staff to them as appropriate

- always maintain confidentiality, unless permission has been given to break it.

References and Further Reading

Field, L and Drysdale, D (1991) *Training for Competence*, Kogan Page, London.

Fletcher, S (1992) *NVQs: Standards and Competence*, (2nd edn), Kogan Page, London.

Hargreaves, PM (1995) *The Training Officer: A Cost-effective Role in a Science Research Organization*, unpublished PhD thesis, University of Surrey.

McLagan, P (1983) *Models for Excellence: The Conclusions and Recommendations of the ASTD Training and Development Competency Study*, American Society for Training and Development Press, Washington, DC.

Saunders, M and Holdaway, K (1992) *The In-House Trainer as Consultant*, Kogan Page, London.

Woolfe, R, Murgatroyd, S and Rhys, S (1987) *Guidance and Counselling in Adult and Continuing Education: A Developmental Perspective*, Open University Press, Milton Keynes.

Chapter 11

Managing the staff developer's role

In the previous three chapters we have provided brief outlines of some of the various roles performed by staff developers together with a few examples of tasks that are performed within these different roles. This complex role, however, itself needs managing and this is the focus of the present chapter.

Since the staff developers have a variety of different roles to perform, they have a degree of freedom to perform their overall task in their own manner – they construct their own role. This freedom has both advantages and disadvantages. The benefits lie in the opportunities the staff developers have to fulfil their own potential in a demanding job. The problems lie in the fact that the pressures put on the staff developer from all sides of the organization generate their own conflicts and stresses.

Role conflict and role strain

Not surprisingly, from time to time, there may be temporary difficulties in managing the job due to the demands made upon staff developers from all sides. This generates role conflict. This problem can be exacerbated when staff developers do not work full-time in their role as is often the case in small and medium-sized businesses. The priorities in the allocation of time to the various activities and demands are not always self-evident. For example, they may have two part-time jobs, such as Personal Assistant to the Management Team and also Staff Developer. On the one hand, they may need to spend a large proportion of time assisting the directors and shareholders in their goal of making a profit, but as staff developers they are still required to counsel staff who feel that they are being pressurized to work harder.

Sometimes line managers or project managers also experience role conflict. Often they recognize the need to provide funds for staff development but cannot do so because they have to prioritize in favour of other needs in their department, eg a new computer. Thus there may be real conflict for fund-holders. Staff developers, as needs analysts, might acknowledge staff needs but as budget holders they may be unable to provide vocational training. In order to resolve this conflict they may feel obliged to spend more time seeking additional funds, etc or look for additional low-cost resources.

Conflict can sometimes take other forms. Sometimes staff will tend to 'drag their heels' and either refuse to participate in staff development activities or find reasons why they should drop out. Staff developers should ensure that places are filled, so that courses are run cost-effectively. On the other hand, they should try to respond to the wishes of staff in their choice of subject matter to be learned if it is likely to help them in their work. Sometimes there may also be an element of role strain in that the work overload within a single task, single role or dual roles may tend to occur because of lack of time or lack of funds.

Organizations should remain aware of this aspect of the job and do what they can to reduce role conflict, role strain and overload. Ultimately, role conflict reduces job satisfaction and adds to the stress.

Coping with stress

Everyone has to cope with stress at some time in their lives but staff developers have to be especially careful to seek ways of reducing it, for example, by working within reasonably well-defined areas as agreed with the management team and deciding on their priorities, roles and tasks. This will help to reduce role strain and role overload. Some ways to help reduce stress are shown:

- get plenty of exercise
- eat healthy foods
- get plenty of sleep
- take breaks – have a chat, a few days' holiday
- relax – smile – it helps
- use humour to reduce a tense situation
- acquire a wide range of skills – it is more easy to be self-reliant
- develop an enthralling hobby
- set yourself realistic deadlines
- talk to a sympathetic, experienced manager, welfare officer or director if you have problems in getting things done
- value friendship.

If a situation becomes too stressful it is best to discuss the situation with a member of the management team.

Time management

Staff developers have to manage a complex role within a relatively short allotted time because training initiatives often involve deadlines! There are a number of ways to ensure that time is well managed and some of them revolve around the following questions:

- Are the difficult tasks tackled first?
- Are lists of things that must be done within the next 24 hours made and adhered to?
- Are lists of priorities prepared and worked to?

Try to ensure that difficult tasks are not shelved. Staff developers clearly set their own agenda to help to ensure that time is used wisely and that role conflict is reduced. There are many ways to save time. Here are a few:

- define goals (with the help of the management team if necessary)
- set a time budget for your activities
- delegate where possible, eg arrange for someone else to do the filing
- put most of your training data on computer
- use e-mail
- negotiate time limits on personal interviews
- remain firm with calls from sales people seeking to sell their training courses. Some may be worthwhile, others not. Check out their literature during a spare moment at a later date
- organize time-management courses for staff and attend one
- improve your reading skills, so that some literature can be scanned while others are read more deeply.

Communication skills

One of the roles of the training officer is to be a good communicator, since this helps to avoid misunderstanding and conflict:

- Look for the most efficient means of communicating within the organization.
- Communicate training-related information to everyone who needs to know but maintain confidentiality where necessary.
- Listen to what people have to say.
- Remain aware that staff developers can convey management policy from the boardroom down to staff of all grades.
- Do not spread gossip but do reassure staff that the management team has their welfare at heart.
- Remove any real or imaginary barriers to communication.

- Keep staff up-to-date with training matters by e-mail, newsletters, etc.
- Obtain the support of the management team to organize cross-department seminars, eg on 'marketing','customer care', new products, new research, etc and encourage everyone to attend them.
- Organize seminars on general work-related topics just for less experienced staff who might be too embarrassed to ask questions in front of their bosses.
- Remain aware that body language provides important signals to others, eg smiling, eye contact, tone of voice, sense of humour.
- Check on information before passing it to others.

Role management

In the light of the wide variety of roles and tasks that the staff developers undertake, it is necessary for them to work out their own priorities and concerns, so that they create a role which they find satisfying and which is also manageable in the context of their work. Therefore, we would suggest that staff developers reading this book should examine the list of roles in Chapter 7 and prioritize them for themselves. We have included a few of the questions that might help HRD personnel carry out an audit of their own role:

- What do you actually do?
- How do you see your role?
- How do your immediate superiors see your role?
- What expectations do the staff have about you?
- What do you think that you do best?
- In what areas do you need to spend more time?
- In what areas do you need further training?
- What are your priorities?
- What is most meaningful to you about your job?
- To what extent do your priorities and most meaningful elements fit into the expectations others have of you?
- What are the emerging priorities in your own company for the staff developer?
- How does the role you play fit into your own system of values?
- How can you make your role more enjoyable to yourself, useful to your organization and beneficial to the staff with whom you work?
- How does what you do fit into your job specification?

These questions are posed in a sequential order, although staff developers might want to reorder them, omit some and include others, in order to make this audit more useful.

When the job is such a diverse one, as the staff developer's is, it is very useful for role players to audit themselves in such a way, that they can be more confident about what they stand for and know what they are trying to achieve.

This chapter has tried to provide some guidance to staff developers about:

- how they create their own role
- how they manage their role
- how they reduce role conflict and strain
- how they can audit themselves.

It is too easy to let the external pressures determine precisely what staff developers should do, especially when they are always seeking to respond to many demands and perform a multitude of tasks in a very limited period of time.

In this part we have produced an overall picture of the most significant functions that staff developers perform. We recognize that there are a great many pressures to chase every possible expectation and that staff developers may feel frustrated because too many functions are being performed and none done as well as they would like to perform them. However, this is not only a chance to self-assess, this book is about how some of the major tasks of human resource specialists may be performed, so that in Part 3 we examine the practical aspects of implementing the training cycle and share ideas about the day-to-day functioning of the staff development department.

Staff developers should ensure that:

- they discuss with the management team the depth of their role and the way in which it should be enacted

- they avoid role conflict

- they avoid role strain

- their work is beneficial to managers and staff

- they enjoy their work and derive satisfaction from it.

References and Further Reading

Adair, J (1988) *Effective Time Management*, Pan Books, London.
Buzan, T (1997) *Speed Reading*, Buzan Centre, Bournemouth.
Cranwell-Ward, J (1987) *Managing Stress*, Gower, Aldershot.
Garratt, S (1994) *Manage your Time*, HarperCollins, London.
Jarvis, P (1985) *The Sociology of Adult and Continuing Education*, Croom Helm, London.

Pettigrew, AM, Jones, GR and Reason, PW (1982) *Training and Development Roles in their Organisational Setting*, Manpower Services Commission Training Division, London.
Pinto, PR and Walker, JW (1978) *A Study of Professional Training and Developmental Roles and Competences*, American Society for Training and Development, Baltimore, MD.
Scott, B (1986) *The Skills of Communicating*, Gower, Aldershot.

PART 3

The training function

Chapter 12

Practical and systematic approach to training

In this chapter we examine a training cycle which provides a guide to the order in which initiatives are implemented. We then focus on a needs analysis and on developing a core curriculum or programme. In the following chapters we examine aspects of managing the whole training function, implementation and evaluation of training.

The cycle of training

As discussed previously, there are four main stages to the training cycle:

- identification of organizational and staff development needs
- decision-making with regard to a core curriculum, training objectives and design of programmes
- implementation of staff development programmes including training delivery
- evaluation of the total staff development activity.

We have listed some of the practical applications linked to each stage of the training cycle in Figure 12.1. For example, interviewing skills are needed when analysing training needs and evaluating training events, while writing skills are required when designing and implementing programmes. Many other skills are required throughout the cycle.

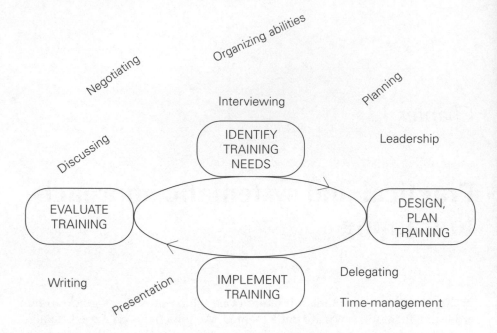

Figure 12.1   *Some practical applications linked to stages of the training cycle (some applications will be necessary throughout the cycle)*

First steps: undertaking a training needs analysis

Information on the needs of the organization and the individual can be obtained from a number of sources, ie from appraisal forms, from discussions with members of the management team, line managers, project managers and individual staff. A needs analysis entails interviewing staff and managers to determine which courses or other training initiatives are likely to be of benefit to them or their groups, teams, departments, etc, for example:

- several managers might benefit from a course on 'interpersonal skills'
- electronics specialists might apply for refresher courses
- sales staff might like to participate in a marketing seminar
- a department, group or team would perhaps benefit from a team-building course.

It is up to the staff developer to find out how such individuals or groups can be helped to develop their skills further. Before beginning a needs analysis, staff developers should have a broad overview on the subject matter that courses or seminars can provide (see Appendix A for some types of courses currently available). Often line managers or other staff are unsure about what the various courses offer and so they will expect staff developers to know broadly which type of initiatives are available, how valuable they might be and whether they are run locally, etc. As a picture of the needs begins to emerge, staff developers should obtain more specific knowledge about the subject matter provided by various training initiatives.

When undertaking needs analyses, consult with all members of staff starting with directors and line managers, but include health and safety officers and trade union staff. When talking to individual staff do not expect them to know precisely what training they want. Some less experienced staff, for instance, may be unaware of their staff development needs so staff developers might recommend that these should be discussed with line managers. On the other hand, some individuals know precisely which courses are useful because of their concerns or interests. They may also have heard their colleagues talking about courses that they have enjoyed. Others may need to be motivated to attend any form of course. Always keep a record of:

• all the requests made by the senior management team
• all the suggestions and ideas put forward
• all the departmental requests from line managers
• all the personal interests and needs expressed by staff.

Training needs may be split into organizational and individual needs but in practice both types result in individual members of staff being trained in a wide variety of subjects.

Organizational needs

An organization might decide to adopt a variety of relatively long-term strategies including:

• a recruitment drive
• development of new products
• some redundancy or pre-retirement initiatives
• development of new technology, including IT
• retraining of staff
• development of new departments
• development of new teams.

There may also be a requirement to train many of their staff so as to:

• improve health and safety
• improve productivity
• improve quality
• improve communication

- improve marketing techniques
- develop creativity
- reduce absenteeism.

The first steps are to consult with the management team to discuss and develop a long-term training strategy and then discuss the subject matter and the time-scales involved. Members of the management team may decide that large-scale training initiatives should be implemented but may be unaware of the implications. To help them to decide on the level of broad-based training needed, staff developers should prepare a report for the management team so that its members can decide whether to implement and support a large-scale training programme. Detail the following for each type of course needed, eg vocational, management development, personal development. Provide details of:

- various titles within each type and its broad objectives
- length of course
- number of staff who would be required to participate
- resources needed, eg rooms, equipment, tutors
- broad estimate of cost – residential or non-residential
- feasibility of running some initiatives in-house
- other implications.

Job-related needs

Usually line managers analyse tasks to determine the level of skills needed by staff and inform staff developers about their unit's training needs. It is essential that staff developers maintain good relationships with all line managers, or else staff in that unit might not have the training opportunities that they require. A further step is to decide which people will need training for particular occupations, eg new recruits, how many and who takes priority.

Staff developers should consult with line managers who are usually knowledgeable about job descriptions and the tasks required. (Sometimes they may be required to analyse the skills, knowledge and attitudes required of a particular job but this should be done in conjunction with line managers.) It will be necessary to ensure that new recruits are conversant with the skills required for a particular job and that longer-serving staff can update their skills. Staff developers should also know about impending promotions so that they can help with additional training when necessary.

Individual needs

Individual needs are usually ongoing and arranged via line managers. Some nominations reach the training department frequently from a variety of sources while others may be outlined by staff or line managers during annual performance appraisals. It is important for staff developers to know as many individuals as possible in the organization, so that they can talk to them and get to know the types of training needs that they feel they have, since what workers feel they need might not always be known to the line manager. Remember also that if staff do not trust their line managers entirely, they might seek to withhold their training needs from them through fear of being thought incompetent, etc. Human resource specialists can overcome some of these problems, so long as they are frequent visitors to all parts of the organization. Sometimes staff themselves may request courses during day-to-day (sometimes confidential) discussions with staff developers. Staff developers should ensure that:

- line managers are willing to nominate staff for training if there is a requirement for it regardless of race, creed, age or gender if funds permit
- less experienced staff are made aware of opportunities for staff development
- union officials are consulted. In many instances individual staff are able to inform staff developers of their precise needs for updating their current skills, eg computing requirements. However, some individuals may need help to define their needs
- academic or practical standards required should be discussed with line managers. Different people may need to be trained in different aspects of a given initiative. For example, several catering staff may require an interpersonal skills course designed for customer care, while the director of a large research organization may require a one-off interpersonal skills course at senior level designed to help her/him to cope with organizing research staff and their projects, so that two different courses would be needed.

Undertaking needs analysis is a complex job but it is one that should be undertaken frequently and staff developers should plan to do this on a regular basis – perhaps by having a timetable for visiting each line manager and all department staff. Doing this regularly is time-consuming but it can prove most useful. An example of an extract of a needs analysis for six staff within a team is shown in Figure 12.2.

Proactivity

In assessing individual needs it is best for staff developers to talk to as many people as they can about their staff development needs:

- remember that people are usually very busy so it often pays to give prior warning of a visit, so that they can be thinking about their own needs and that of their staff

Individual Needs

Name	Initials	Staff No.	Grade	Dept.	Type of course needed	Preferred course title or comments	Date
Griffin	T.D.	23445	P.A.	Finance	Information on Internet	One at local centre	5.5.98
Wooler	B.K.	23391	Sen Manager	Finance	Financial Management	in-house – linked to present software	5.5.98
Johnson	D.P.	23813	Research Asst	R & D	Computer Programming	One run at local college	6.5.98
Johnson	D.P.	23813	Research Asst	R & D	Technical Writing	In-house if possible	6.5.98
Hancock	F.O.	23782	Tech. Eng III	R & D	Advanced Welding	Same course as colleagues	6.5.98
Strong	J.V.	23458	Project Eng. II	R & D	Project Management	Computer-based	6.5.98
Denyer	J.S.	23551	Salesman	Publicity	Advanced French	Advanced conversation	7.5.98

Figure 12.2 An extract from a needs analysis

- remain aware that although some managers will devote an hour or more per month to such discussion, most will have time only for a few minutes
- keep an 'open door' to your office so that people can call in to see you to discuss their training needs.

Undertaking this role requires that staff developers should have good interviewing and communication skills.

Interviewing skills

Interviewing skills should be developed so that staff find it easy to talk about their aspirations and are motivated to participate in education and training. In some instances individuals may need help to define or articulate their needs. Staff developers may therefore need other data and information about individuals' education and previous work experience and skill levels in order to help them. Consequently, staff developers should acquire a number of basic skills in this aspect of their work. Interviewing skills include the following:

- listening to what people have to say
- allowing plenty of time for individuals to discuss their training needs or other related topics
- understanding how the other person feels
- showing empathy
- understanding cultural and sub-cultural differences
- being willing to learn in the interaction.

A core curriculum or programme

Once organizational, job-related and individual needs have been listed, it is possible to decide on a core curriculum, ie those initiatives which should be on offer to everyone within the organization if they are broadly relevant to their job. Developing a core curriculum is not a clear-cut exercise and it is essentially a dynamic exercise. Some of the training initiatives listed in the core curriculum might change from year to year. For example, the core curriculum may include:

- finance training for fund-holders and project managers
- management skills for all management staff
- presentational skills for all staff involved with training others, marketing for public relations staff or others involved in making presentations
- interpersonal skills
- training in first aid for departmental representatives

- team training for all departments
- regular intra-departmental seminars
- informal in-house discussion groups
- basic health and safety programme for all staff, whatever their level within the organization
- job refresher courses.

Computerized database

Nominations for organizational and individual training needs accumulate surprisingly rapidly so they should be entered onto a computerized spread sheet and backed up daily. Each entry may take the form of a row of information giving the following:

- name of member of staff
- staff number
- grade
- department
- type of course needed
- preferred course title
- date of request.

(See Figure 12.2.) For example, one person may have two entries if he or she is nominated for two different courses. There are different formats for entering data depending on the design of the software available. Most will cope with hundreds of entries. Specific software for entering training data is available commercially and if there are large numbers of people in the organization it may be worth investing in a package.

Completing the final analysis of organizational, job and individual training

Staff developers should collate a final list of staff and the initiatives for which they are nominated and then prioritize the needs. The next step is to consider the ways of matching training needs with particular types of courses for particular groups of people, followed by planning and developing a timetable of training events. This should include:

- long-term or short-term training events
- in-house or external training initiatives
- work-based 'at the desk or bench' initiatives or 'classroom' based training.

Often it is best to plan a provisional timetable initially and to finalize it later when bookings/places etc are confirmed. Planning a timetable when designing programmes is discussed in more detail in Chapter 13. In Chapter 14 we discuss the compilation of a training calendar.

Although some short-term initiatives may be planned and implemented within a few weeks, long-term or specialized education and training should be planned at least six months to one or two years ahead (for example, degree courses or exchange visits). Decisions have to be made on whether it is best to design initiatives to be run in-house or to employ consultants. As an alternative it may be better to use pre-existing courses either in-house or via external training organizations.

The design of training initiatives and the range of methods which are available are discussed in the next chapter. The practicalities of matching training needs to supply are discussed thereafter.

Staff developers should:

- ensure that they, the management teams or line managers inform staff of the long-term training plans, giving the reasons for the various initiatives and the time-scales involved

- ensure that training is conducted within a time-scale which is reasonably acceptable to staff and their line managers

- consult with all staff about their own training needs and those of their assistants

- consult with other interest groups

- so far as possible adopt an equal opportunities policy for staff of similar grades

- plan well ahead.

References and Further Reading

Boydell, TH (1990) *A Guide to the Identification of Training Needs*, Department of Education and Employment, London.

Fletcher, S (1991) *NVQs: Standards and Competence*, (2nd edn), Kogan Page, London.

Further Education Unit (1987) *Planning Staff Development: A Guide for Managers*, Further Education Unit, London.

Hall, DT and Associates, (1986) *Career Development in Organizations*, Jossey-Bass, San Francisco.

Hunt, JW (1990) Management development for the year 2000, *Journal of Management Development*, 9(3):4–13.

Jessup, G (1991) *Outcomes: NVQs and the Emerging Model of Education and Training*, Falmer, London.

Kenney, J and Reid, M (1986) *Training Interventions*, Institute of Personnel Management, London.

Management Charter Initiative (1990) *Management Development in Action*, Management Charter Initiative, London.

Mumford, A (1988) *Developing Top Managers*, Gower, Aldershot.

Payne, J (1991) *Women, Training and the Skills Shortage: The Case for Public Investment*, Policy Studies Institute, London.

Pearson, P and Heyno, A (1988) *Helping the Unemployed Professional*, John Wiley, Chichester.

Pepper, AD (1992) *Managing the Training and Development Function*, (2nd edn), Gower, Aldershot.

Peterson, R (1992) *Training Needs Analysis in the Workplace*, Kogan Page, London.

Chapter 13

Practical aspects of programme design

In the previous chapter we discussed the work of staff developers in compiling and analysing staff needs where we saw that, in some instances, it is necessary to design in-house training programmes especially if:

- it is more cost-effective to do so
- a particular initiative is not available 'off the shelf'
- the initiative needs to be tailored to the specific needs of the organization or its staff.

Programme design

In Chapter 9 we discussed the roles of programme designers and outlined basic points on which a programme design is based, including the identification of learning objectives. We are now going to look at some of the practicalities of this undertaking and discuss some of the teaching and learning methods that can be incorporated into such programmes. A well-known US educator of adults, C O Houle (1972) suggested that in designing the format it is necessary to consider the following points:

- resources
- leaders
- methods
- schedule
- sequence
- social reinforcement

- individualization
- roles and relationships
- criteria for evaluation
- clarity of design.

We will look at these individually.

Resources

We have already emphasized this. It is necessary to have the funding, the premises and the equipment necessary to produce the programme.

Leaders

It is essential that the correct and properly qualified leaders or teachers or trainers be employed to undertake the programme. Consequently, it is wise for staff developers to have a bank of acceptable tutors or trainers, with some notes about their availability and expertise.

Methods

It is important to recognize that there are a wide variety of methods that can be employed and 'variety is the spice of life'! Such programmes may be in the normal classroom situation, in the workplace or even by self-directed learning methods. Account should be taken of how adults learn, as we have already discussed, but also whether the topic is best learned through teaching, work-based instruction or through a self-directed learning package. This is among the first decisions that needs to be taken in programme planning. Thereafter, other decisions need to be made about the teaching method. If, for instance, it is to be in the normal classroom situation, it must be recalled that there are a wide variety of teaching or training methods and it is essential that variation be brought into any course. There is a tendency either to have all lectures, all syndicate groups, all courses, etc, whereas there is a wide variety of teaching methods (see Jarvis, 1995).

Schedule

Often the time schedule is set by the way that the company works but staff developers need to ensure that the proposed timetable facilitates attendance at the planned event and it is wise to discuss the timing with the relevant personnel, eg line managers, while it is still in the planning stage.

Sequence

Whether the training event is a single day or at a number of separate times, it is necessary to ensure that the content sequence is well planned, so that there are logical connections between them.

Social reinforcement

It is necessary that those who participate feel that their participation has been worthwhile, either to themselves personally or to the organization, etc. Staff developers should ensure that there is always positive reinforcement of this nature given to all the participants.

Individualization

Each worker is unique, a human being who is coming, or has come, on a training event. They ought to be made to feel their own individuality during the training, rather than merely being another number, a member of staff, etc. Usually events are designed for optimum numbers of people.

Roles and relationships

People on training events come from a variety of different positions in the organization. Consequently, it is always necessary to clarify if this role diversity will enhance or hinder the event. This is sometimes difficult, and there are occasions when senior staff will expect junior staff to remain junior in the training situation. It is necessary to have this well thought out and discussed beforehand. Often, it might be wise to ensure that senior staff will participate fully if junior staff are present and vice versa. Sometimes a more junior member of staff may be the instructor, and senior staff have to learn from those who are in subordinate positions to them in the organization.

Criteria for evaluation

It is necessary to plan these prior to the event – whether the criteria are going to relate to the event itself, to the learning that the participants have gained or the effect that the learning has on the place of work. Naturally, all three could be included, but evaluation is often a difficult business to do well. Often it consists of a questionnaire given at the end of the event – but this tends to be a fairly meaningless exercise! We will look at other approaches later.

Clarity of design

Often people who come to courses say, 'I did not know it was going to be like this!', etc. The training event has to be carefully designed so that staff can be told precisely what the content is, and the methods to be used if they ask. Certainly, if experiential methods are employed, then it is important that staff as intending participants are aware of the types of activity that have been designed into the programme.

Under the heading of 'Contextualizing the Format', Houle discusses a number of features, although for the staff developer only one is of major significance and this is 'guidance and counselling'. Staff developers should always be prepared to give honest advice about whether a planned event is relevant to the needs of any individual who asks. This is one of the reasons why planning needs to be so thorough. A diagrammatic representation of factors involved in programme design is given in Figure 13.1.

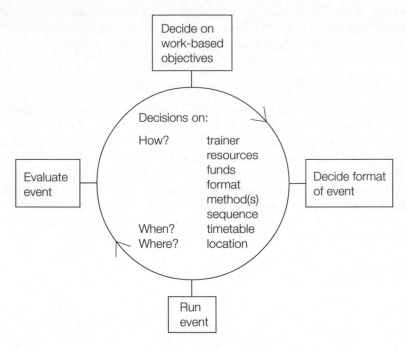

Figure 13.1   *A diagrammatic representation of programme design*

It is always necessary to check with line managers and the management team to make sure that there is a real need for the event and that numbers of staff who are likely to attend are sufficient. Also check whether a suitable location is available with facilities, eg catering, computing facilities, etc.

Use of media

There are now many excellent video tapes on a wide variety of topics which staff developers may include in a course. Audio-visual aids are discussed in Chapter 16. Various media may be used when implementing programmes and these include information technology, films and video tapes. Sometimes the staff developer is able to make short video tapes to explain a point. However, it is usually best to choose from the numerous ready-made tapes, films and computer programmes that cover a wide range of training-related subjects. These can then be run in sequence together with other material. However, staff developers should never use audio-visual material unless they have heard or viewed it beforehand themselves. This is another apparently time-consuming exercise, but it is one which helps avoid mishaps later.

Training objectives

Staff developers also often have to make joint decisions about training objectives and course content with the management team, line managers, unions and other interest groups and with potential participants.

Very frequently, staff developers have been teacher-centred in their course planning, but this is rather traditional and not as effective as that training which is trainee-centred. We have, therefore, already specified that the personal needs of the staff should be considered. There are other factors that also have to be taken into consideration, and these will now be discussed.

Learning styles

It is important for the course designer to:

- take into account the preferred learning styles of individuals or groups of staff (often he or she will reinforce or build on existing learning)
- organize a good mix between tutor input and group input so that participants are strongly involved.

Activities which work well for some staff may not be appropriate for others. For example, senior management staff may well be used to fast-moving discussion and decision-making while less experienced staff may require a longer time for problem-solving.

In some instances where large numbers of people are being trained for a particular job, or courses are designed by consultants, there may be little opportunity for their content to be updated for, perhaps, several months. On the other hand, there may be ample opportunity to change the methods used if they do not seem to be working well. Training methods are discussed further in Chapter 15.

Timing and length of a course

Often staff developers will have to discuss with interested parties the amount of time they can spare employees to be away from the workplace. Consequently, staff developers may have to compromise on the way the course is designed to accommodate the needs of different departments. Thus, it is important to know the minimum amount of time a course will take, as well as the preferred length. For instance, some courses will take a number of days, but would the departments prefer staff to be away in a single block or on day-release? Whether the course is best run for five consecutive days or whether line managers can only release staff for one day a week, over four weeks, etc, are all important considerations.

The timing of a course will also depend on the availability of participants and external tutors. Often an internal training initiative needs to be booked six months to a year in advance in order to obtain specialist tutors and to ensure that participants can make sure that they are free to attend. In a similar manner, it is worth knowing whether a three-hour course would best be run in the morning or the afternoon, etc.

Short-term evaluation and pilot schemes

When courses are designed that will be repeated over a period of time for a large number of people, it is worth implementing a pilot course to check whether:

- the content is relevant and worthwhile
- the sequence of activities are workable
- the expected standards are achievable
- staff are happy to participate in the initiative and feel that other colleagues may also wish to be involved.

Such evaluation tends to become an ongoing process and the staff developer can expect to receive useful and sometimes critical comments about any in-house or external initiatives in which staff participate.

Other factors to consider include:

- choosing from various methods and activities to promote learning
- sequencing the activities

- deciding whether audio-visual material should be incorporated
- deciding when and where a course should be delivered
- deciding who should deliver it – are specialist speakers required?
- deciding on the way it should be marketed.

Deciding on the timetable for a course

It is important to plan the daily or weekly timetable for each course so that various factors are taken into account:

- teaching methods which fit in with preferred methods of learning by participants, eg student-centred
- time for introductions at the start of a course so that participants get to know each other
- there is at least one easy icebreaker at the start
- the right mix of theory and practice occurs. This will depend on the objectives and standards for the course
- time for refreshment or meal breaks is allowed
- there is time for a few minutes' relaxation at lunch or tea-time, eg a walk, telephone call, etc
- the provision of books or software for further studies.

Managing resources and compiling a timetable is discussed in the next chapter.

It is clear from all that we have looked at so far, that staff developers do not have total freedom to design and manage their programmes as there are numerous factors involved. Thus, in the following chapter, we want to explore ways that training might be managed.

Staff developers should:

- be systematic in the design and preparation of programmes

- take many factors into account when designing initiatives

- take preferred methods of learning into account – staff usually know which suits them best

- evaluate training materials once a design is complete

- pilot large-scale schemes, wherever possible.

References and Further Reading

Brookfield, SD (1986) *Understanding and Facilitating Adult Learning*, Jossey-Bass, San Francisco.

Corder, C (1990) *Teaching Hard, Teaching Soft*, Gower, Aldershot.

Further Education Unit, (1987) *Planning Staff Development: A Guide for Managers*, Further Education Unit, London.

Honey, P and Mumford, A (1986) *The Manual of Learning Styles*, (2nd edn), Peter Honey, Maidenhead.

Houle, CO (1972) *The Design of Education*, Jossey-Bass, San Francisco.

Jarvis, P (1995) *Adult and Continuing Education: Theory and Practice*, (2nd edn), Routledge, London.

Leigh, DA (1991) *Practical Approach to Group Training*, Kogan Page, London.

Wiggs, GD (1984) Designing Learning Programs, in Nadler, L (ed.), *The Handbook of Human Resource Development*, John Wiley, New York, pp. 7.1–7.35.

Chapter 14

Managing the training function

In Chapter 12 we discussed some of the practical aspects of undertaking a needs analysis for individuals within the organization. In this chapter we discuss the practicalities of managing the training function to ensure its smooth running. One of the most vital aspects is to match training needs with supply, ensuring that staff are trained at the right time to certain standards so that not only can they do their job efficiently and effectively but also so that they can develop their own capabilities and opportunities for self-advancement. This requires the application of several aspects:

- maintaining good public relations
- negotiating for sponsorship and funding
- negotiating for other resources
- deciding on training options
- hiring consultants to give in-house training
- selecting or confirming participants for courses
- compiling a calendar of training events
- marketing training initiatives.

Each of these will now be discussed in turn.

Maintaining good public relations

It is important to build up a good relationship between the training department and other departments within the organization and to understand the point of view of managers of other departments and their staff. They are the main customers of the Human Resources Department. It is very worthwhile to invest time to network with all the departments and to persuade them to support the training department in their day-to-day activities. They also need to feel involved in what the training department does. Consult with them when planning a strategy for training – they may have some new ideas worth trying. Obtain feedback from them about the success or otherwise of your work or department.

Negotiating for sponsorship and funding

Once funding has been agreed, a list of initiatives can be finalized. In some instances, central funds are made available to the training department as part of a contract which requires that a given number of courses will be organized and implemented for a given number of people within the funding level allowed (a type of service level agreement). But, in others, funding needs to be obtained from elsewhere, such as departmental budgets.

In some organizations there are no specific avenues for central funding, and then it is provided by separate departments or groups. In this instance, training departments may require project managers, line managers or other fund-holders to sign letters or forms nominating groups of staff, teams or departments for given training initiatives.

Following periodic discussions about organizational or job training needs and where large numbers of staff have to be trained, the training department should request a confirmatory letter from each department which should:

- specify the types of course needed by each individual
- specify the standards required
- indicate the source of funding.

Nomination forms

Departments should nominate staff to attend specific functions and it is wise to have a special nomination form. These are normally used to confirm one-off requests arising from an individual need although, in practice, nomination forms may be received from departments at any time of the year.

An example of a nomination form which should be signed by a nominee and her or his line manager is given in Figure 14.1. Each form is then retained for the use of the training department or subsequently by trainers or tutors. It should include the following information:

- name of potential participant
- name of type of course, eg time management
- preferred location
- preference for local or residential course

TRAINING NOMINATION FORM

SURNAME: ....

FORENAMES: ....

TITLE: Dr/Mr/Mrs/Miss/Ms .... GRADE: .... PAY NUMBER: ....

AGE: .... (if under 18) ....LENGTH OF SERVICE: ....

NAME OF ORGANIZATION: ....

EMPLOYING DEPARTMENT: ....

YOUR OFFICE TELEPHONE NUMBER: .... YOUR E-MAIL ADDRESS: ....

COURSE REQUIRED: ....

PREFERRED LOCATION: ....

....

RESIDENTIAL OR NON-RESIDENTIAL COURSE PREFERRED?: ....

PREFERRED DATES/TIME OF YEAR: ....

REASONS FOR PARTICIPATING IN THE COURSE: ....

OVERLEAF PLEASE GIVE BROAD DETAILS OF EDUCATIONAL QUALIFICATIONS AND PREVIOUS COURSES ATTENDED DURING LAST TWO YEARS

NOMINEE'S SIGNATURE: .... DATE: ....

_____

MAXIMUM COST ALLOWED FOR COURSE: ....

SOURCE OF FUNDING: ....

LINE MANAGER'S COMMENTS: ....

LINE MANAGER'S SIGNATURE: .... DATE: ....

Figure 14.1 *An example of a training nomination form*
Source: Joint Training Service (NERC) (permission obtained)

- approximate funds available to cover the approximate cost of the course plus travel, hotel costs, taxes, etc
- brief details of educational background
- reasons for participating in the course.

All of this information can be made available to course tutors later, although if personal details are to be made known to the tutors, then it is wise to specify that fact on the form.

It is imperative that nomination forms, which represent an internal contract, are signed. They perform several functions. They:

- request or confirm a training need
- represent an agreement between line managers and potential participants and the training department
- specify the type of training needed
- confirm that it will be funded and at what level
- provide information about the previous work or training experience of the potential participant which will be of use to a course tutor
- help to provide the staff developer with a reasonable estimate of the numbers of places needed on given staff development initiatives.

Negotiating for other resources

Sometimes it may be possible to borrow equipment or to participate in subsidized training schemes, for example, government-sponsored training for young people. To augment training resources, it is worthwhile:

- exploring all avenues to obtain funds from the organization, project managers, fund-holders, line managers
- enquiring to see if there are any subsidized training schemes in the local area, eg government-sponsored modern apprenticeships for young people, the unemployed, etc
- investigating bursaries or sponsorship provided by professional organizations.

Final costs of training initiatives

It is important to estimate final costs of courses (including any taxes), seminars, workshops, etc, and to confirm that funds are available from the organization for all of the training initiatives listed. Organizational funds may vary throughout the year and sometimes loss of external business contracts means loss of funds for training! Final decisions on the level of staff development and who shall provide it during any one year will depend mainly on the amount of funding available and the availability of staff to participate. The better the reputation of the training department, the easier it is to gain support for its activities.

Deciding on training options

Decisions about matching training needs with supply depend on a wide range of factors including numbers of staff likely to attend specific sessions, training objectives, standards required, expertise available, resources needed, accommodation, costs, the time needed to train, recommendations of line managers, peer groups, trade unions, health and safety requirements. These all have to be taken into consideration and prioritized during programme planning at the start of each year.

Types of course currently available

Many of the types of course currently available in the UK may be categorized as follows:

- developing an organization
- financial management
- health and safety
- information technology
- managing projects
- managing staff
- quality control
- sales and marketing
- self-development, eg time management, languages
- vocational.

In addition, competency-based national curricula for various occupations are available from the Qualifications and Curriculum Authority in the UK.

There are numerous commercial courses available, to which staff can gain access and these can be delivered via a variety of different modes. Indeed, there are too many to list here, even if it were possible to gather all the information. However, some examples of titles are given in Appendix A.

Selecting from options

When deciding on which course to follow, the options open to the training department are to:

- decide that 'on-the-job' vocational training is the best option (eg 'sitting next to Nellie')
- decide to implement such programmes as seminars, lectures, workshops, mentoring, job-exchange with a view to improving expertise, problem-solving and communication
- decide to implement participation in formal schemes, such as National Vocational Qualifications or other nationally recognized modem apprenticeships
- design courses to be run in-house which match training needs in terms of objectives and standards, eg presentation skills
- consult with competent external organizations with a view to arranging part of the training programme to be run externally, where appropriate. This is a useful option for specialized courses, such as management development or vocational and technical training sometimes offered by manufacturers, eg electronics
- call in a consultant or other specialist with a view to designing and arranging courses in-house.

Estimating

Often staff developers have to decide whether to book staff on pre-arranged external courses or design specialized courses to be run in-house. Decisions are based on how many participants are involved and the subject in which they will receive training:

- If there are few trainees, it may be cheaper to send them on external courses.
- If large numbers are involved, it may be best to design in-house courses.
- It may be cheaper and more effective to employ specialist trainers to run courses in-house rather than to send staff to external organizations for training.
- Specialist equipment and expertise required may be only available externally.
- Other excellent alternatives for staff development include short- or long-term open learning or distance learning (provided by many universities or colleges or other educational institutes).

Factors to take into account when deciding on in-house options

There are a number of factors that need to be considered when designing an in-house training programme, such as whether there are:

- sufficient good instructors available
- sufficient participants

- other alternatives available
- specialists or consultants available to advise on content. They can often implement particular training objectives within a course, seminar or workshop.

It is perhaps very important to recognize that a number of the very large companies in the United States, and now in the UK, are actually establishing very high level in-house training facilities, and even calling them corporate universities. These are establishing reputations for high quality teaching and learning.

Factors to take into account when deciding on external options

Likewise, there are factors that need to be taken into account when considering the external options:

- costs
- resources available
- location
- length of initiative
- standard of accommodation
- ambience of the location
- facilities for disabled participants
- whether health and safety standards will be enforced
- academic standards or level of competence to be achieved
- qualifications or credibility of trainers
- previous recommendations.

If large numbers of participants from the company are involved, then it may be best to design in-house courses, although they also have a number of disadvantages.

Disadvantages of in-house initiatives

- interruptions from non-participants or line managers
- participants may become involved with their daily work
- unless special training rooms are permanently available, space may be limited
- staff developers will need to spend more time finalizing details of the whole event, eg catering, seminar rooms
- specialist training aids may have to be borrowed or hired.

Thus, there are a number of advantages for having external programmes.

Advantages of external initiatives

- can be residential
- full catering facilities are usually available
- purpose-built, fully equipped seminar or conference rooms
- staff may feel that they are better able to discuss sensitive issues away from the work environment
- no interruptions from people in the workplace
- staff may be less concerned about their day-to-day work
- may be less time-consuming for the training department.

At the same time, external programmes, especially residential ones, do have disadvantages.

Disadvantages of external initiatives

- staff, particularly those with domestic responsibilities, may not be happy to attend residential courses
- may involve long-distance travel
- usually more expensive
- often have to be booked well in advance – sometimes up to a year.

It is worth remembering that many courses are available through distance learning, CD ROM and even on the Web, and there are advantages and disadvantages of courses such as these.

Advantages of distance learning

- can be undertaken in own time
- can be studied at own pace
- can be studied at home or at work
- sometimes it is cheaper.

Disadvantages of distance learning

- often it is studied alone and sometimes it is easy to lose motivation
- nobody to discuss the material with, especially if there are things that staff cannot understand
- sometimes the course is not entirely relevant, or has become dated
- companies might expect staff to undertake their training in their own time.

It is significant that the Labour Government in the UK is at present investigating the possibilities of a University for Industry, seeking already established courses, approving them and making them widely available. Staff developers should follow these events closely and, if given opportunities, contribute to the debate about the way that this might develop.

Hiring consultants to give in-house training

Many companies do not have sufficient in-house expertise and have to use external consultants. There are no restrictions on people calling themselves consultants and offering their services to whosoever will purchase them. Staff developers should therefore always be careful about employing external people:

- Always interview consultants, trainers or teachers before you make a decision about taking them on to help with the training function. Usually another member of staff or someone from the personnel department, especially with subject expertise, should be asked to assist in the initial interview.
- Remember the reputation of training and the training department relies on the choices being made.
- Usually employ well qualified or very experienced trainers or consultants.
- Ensure that they are flexible and prepared to fit in with the culture of the organization, even if they are on very short-term contracts.
- Ask for curriculum vitae.
- Obtain references of both a personal and professional nature – these should be up-to-date and impeccable.
- Make sure that the consultant is prepared to abide by health and safety legislation.
- Consult other departments in order to get help in establishing a potential consultant's credentials.
- Ensure the Personnel Department undertakes the formal hiring arrangements, contracts, etc.

Having selected consultants or specialist trainers to run courses or other initiatives, well in advance, ensure that there is agreement between the staff developer and the consultant about:

- training objectives
- general standard expected of participants
- content and process of the course
- methods to be used for evaluation.

If they are only coming as instructors, they also need to know:

- participants' level of seniority and their previous experience
- location of training centre with map

- dates, times and duration of courses
- resources and equipment available.

Negotiating fees

When contacting consultants or taking on tutors or trainers to run in-house or external training initiatives, it is often possible to negotiate fees, depending on the number of courses to be run. Staff developers are purchasers of services in this respect and should ensure that they get value for money. Ensure that written quotations or agreements are obtained for the following and pass a copy of these to the company accountant or cashier:

- fees per consultant, trainer or tutor for each course, seminar, etc
- the length of each course
- the standard of the course and possible certification resulting from it
- their travel and subsistence costs
- costs of teaching aids and equipment, eg video tapes, computers
- costs of books, disks and hand-outs – these can be expensive
- any taxes which might be payable
- the number of participants each consultant is prepared to take on each course.

Selecting or confirming participants for courses

Although the training department might have the names of potential participants for courses, confirmation should always be sought from all potential participants when planning a course. There are several factors to consider as shown:

- What is the optimum numbers of trainees required for any given course?
- Participants may have a preference for either residential or non-residential courses.
- Participants or their line managers will have a preference for a particular course content.
- Participants will need to know the level of the course and the type of award obtained.
- Groups may need to be of broadly similar academic standard, eg for language training.
- Groups may need to be at a particular level of seniority.
- Senior management staff might like to attend a different course than those they employ and vice versa.
- Some participants may intimidate others.

- There may need to be a good mix of males and females or managers and subordinates.
- Some participants may like to attend a course away from others in the organization, eg interpersonal skills.
- Nervous participants, eg new recruits, might wish to attend courses or seminars with colleagues.
- Participants may be unable to travel far.

Booking courses

If the course being arranged is an external one, there are many factors that need to be taken into account prior to confirming the booking. Staff developers should ensure that:

- the aims and objectives of each course match the requirements of staff (ask for an up-to-date brochure)
- the training department has a written undertaking from participants and their line manager that they are able to attend. (Some managers may require up to a year's notice.)
- there is an agreement that the sponsoring department pays for the course in advance (if applicable). If their staff drop out, then the onus is on that department to find a replacement or meet the costs incurred
- bookings for the course are made at the appropriate time – some companies require bookings a year in advance, and some also require full payment at the time of booking. Other training companies may need a short period of notice
- an agreement is reached if bookings are made far ahead, that substitutes can attend if the original named person drops out.

Final arrangements for external events

These are usually made by external firms who will write to the training department or the participants direct to confirm arrangements. But within the organization, the staff developers are responsible for making sure that no hitches occur, so they should check that participants know the time, place and location of the event and that they have received confirmation of booking.

Internal courses

If an in-house training course is intended, staff developers should:

- book participants on it well ahead so that they can plan their time as far ahead as possible for courses, work, family holidays, etc

- if possible, hold a reserve list of three or four participants, informing them of the possibilities of getting on a particular course. Some may be prepared to wait a while
- prepare a folder of information for each participant giving the timetable of the event, with subject matter, dates, times, map of location and facilities
- state whether the event is residential or non-residential.

An example of a timetable for a non-residential in-house course is given in Figure 14.2. Sometimes dinner is provided at the end of each day, if required.

Compiling a calendar of training events

Having decided broadly on the best way of matching training needs with supply, it is important to produce a calendar of events either for the following six months or a year ahead, to include external and internally run initiatives. An example of part of a calendar is shown in Figure 14.3.

At this stage the training department will know roughly the names of potential participants for most courses. However, on the one hand, there are always drop-outs and, on the other, new enquiries or request for courses are often a regular occurrence.

Marketing training initiatives

Often it is necessary to market training initiatives because it is cost-effective to fill all available places. There are often vacancies because:

- there may be cancellations due to sickness, people leaving, etc
- extra places may be made available at the last minute
- free courses or seminars may be organized by other departments, eg finance or computing, with very little notice
- additional space may be made available for seminars
- seminars or lectures, etc, may be open to all without prior booking
- some types of course require a minimum number of participants if they are to be run successfully, eg interpersonal skills
- extra funds may be made available by headquarters of the management team specifically for training their staff.

Additionally, in their role as manager and programme administrator, staff developers have to ensure that tutors and participants are at the right place at the right date and time and that all the necessary documentation and resources are available. Notes on the courses and learning material may need to be sent to participants several weeks beforehand so that they have time to prepare. For example, they may need to prepare a short talk or report.

	MONDAY	TUESDAY	WEDNESDAY	THURSDAY	FRIDAY
9:00		Review Organizational Culture Organizational Style	Review Customer Care/ Managing For Quality	Review Implementing Policy Strategies For Change	Review Discussion Forum with Senior Manager
11:00	Coffee Welcome, Domestics & Introductions Programme Week 3 in Context	Coffee Organizational Conflict	Coffee Customer Care/ Managing For Quality	Coffee Project	Coffee Action Planning
13:00	Lunch	Lunch	Lunch	Lunch	Lunch
14:00	Understanding The Organization Culture	Creativity Developing Power and Influence	Customer Care/ Managing For Quality	Project	
16:00	Tea	Tea	Tea	Tea	
16:30	Organizational Culture Style	Developing Power and Influence	Customer Care/ Managing For Quality	Project	
18:00	Reflection time				

Figure 14.2 *A timetable for a non-residential in-house course*
Source: Joint Training Service (NERC) (permission obtained)

Calendar of in-house Training Events 1998

Course title	Jan	Feb	Mar	April	May	June	July	Aug	Sept	Oct	Nov	Dec
Report Writing (2 days)	20–21					25–26				6–7		
Telephone Techniques (half-day)	9			3				5			30	
Marketing (1 day)			4				10					3
Customer Care (1 day)	3	25			7			18			26	
Management Development (2 days)		18–19		9–10			15–16				13–14	
Public Speaking (2 days)			18–19			4–5			22–23			
Delegation for Managers (1 day)	14				19			29				11
Negotiation for Managers (1 day)			17			15			4			
Seminar: Action Learning (1 day)		3			21				15			
etc.												

Figure 14.3   *Part of a calendar of training events*

Preparation of the lecture or seminar room

Staff developers should prepare the room in advance by:

- checking well beforehand that the equipment needed is available, eg computers, audio-visual monitors, etc.
- ensuring that there are several audio-visual monitors if there is a large audience
- ensuring that the microphones work
- buying several flip charts and placing them permanently in in-house conference and seminar rooms
- ensuring that valuable equipment used for training sessions is secure overnight
- arranging seating to suit the audience – some ideas are given in Chapter 16
- providing paper and pencils for notetaking
- providing plenty of spare timetables – people tend to lose them.

In the next chapter we discuss delivering the actual training.

Staff developers should:

- plan well ahead

- take care that the aims and objectives of the courses match those expected by the trainees

- ensure that all requirements for a training event, ie participants, trainers and material resources are present at the right time, date and location.

References and Further Reading

Adair, J (1983) *Training for Leadership*, Gower, Aldershot.

Corder, C (1990) *Teaching Hard, Teaching Soft*, Gower, Aldershot

Field, L and Drysdale, D (1991) *Training for Competence*, Kogan Page, London.

Holmberg, B and Baath, JA (1982) *Distance Education: A Short Handbook*, LiberHermods, Malmo.

Jarvis, P (1995) *Adult and Continuing Education: Theory and Practice*, (2nd edn), Routledge, London.

Lewis, R (1986) What is open learning?, *Open Learning*, June: 5–10.

Pepper, AD (1984) *Managing the Training and Development Function*, Gower, Aldershot.

Thayer, PW and McGehee, W (1977) On the effectiveness of not holding a formal training course, *Personnel Psychology*, 30:455–6.

Chapter 15

Delivering training

In previous chapters we have looked at the roles of the staff developer 'behind the scenes', ie before they actually implement a training event. We have seen some of the initiatives taken. In this chapter our focus is upon the actual delivery of training, in the situation where the staff developers themselves act as teachers or trainers. We shall look specifically at many different methods, although we would refer staff developers to a textbook on teaching adults in order to develop the various aspect of their work (see, for example, Jarvis, 1995; Rogers; 1989; Jaques, 1991). Using visual aids is the topic of the next chapter.

Delivery of training

Staff developers should only teach those subjects in which they are proficient. There is a temptation, however, to deliver courses in areas in which they are not specialists since it avoids a lot of additional work. However, this is unwise in the long run. Remember 'the medium is the message' in this respect and the staff developer is the key message about training. Not only should they know their material, they should be experts in the variety of methods used to teach adults. We have no intention of repeating all the different methods and techniques here, but we will provide an overview of the preparation and presentation processes.

It must be pointed out that few trainers can conduct many sessions without thorough preparation – people can get by 'on their fat' for a while, but the hard work in teaching and training is in the preparation.

There is a broad sequence of events through which preparation should proceed:

- Learn the material that needs to be taught.
- Decide precisely on the aims and objectives.
- Decide on the sequence of that material.
- Plan the introduction and conclusion.
- Plan the methods that will be used.
- Decide on the audio-visual aids to be used.
- Decide on forms of evaluation to be used and what is to be evaluated.

Content

It is very important that trainers research the material that they want to teach. Even if trainers think that they know it, it is very wise to recheck on everything, so that they have a definite knowledge of the material. Having undertaken the research, it is wise to remember that when we teach experienced adults, there may always be someone at the session who knows as much or more than us about the subject. Hence, we always need to be humble about what we are going to teach, but know it well. As a small teaching point, if that someone in the session is an expert, then use the expert's knowledge by drawing that person into the class and give time for everybody, including the expert, to contribute.

Do not be fooled by the person who just appears to get up and speak without notes, etc. This confidence either comes of ignorance, or of being a genuine expert who has really done the homework and feels confident of being able to hold the group without notes. Indeed, effortless superiority is an image that many people like to present! Superiority is rarely effortless, however, and so it is important that we do our preparation properly.

Aims and objectives

Aim is usually the broad philosophical intention of the whole session or course. It is worth having an overall philosophy about what we are seeking to do during the course or the event.

Objectives are much more specific intentions of what will be achieved during each session. It is wise to work them out. There are roughly two forms of objectives – behavioural and expressive. Despite its popularity, however, the behavioural approach is conceptually very weak and contains questionable moral overtones (see Jarvis, 1997), and so we would like to introduce you to another way of specifying your objectives – process and product objectives.

In preparing the session, trainers should specify what they want the learners/participants to do during the session, ie the process objectives. Clearly, this relates to methods, and we will discuss these next. However, trainers also want the participants to see the sequence of the session, to interact with others, to develop questioning approaches to their learning, to enjoy the process itself.

Therefore, it is useful to specify the types of things to be experienced by the participants during the process of the training event.

However, there are also product objectives. These can be thought of in terms of what we want the participants to have learned by the end of a session – the new knowledge they will have gained, the new skills they will have acquired, the different attitudes they will have gained. Trainers should spell these out also, but take care not to become too ambitious for any single session. They have to remain realistic about what is likely to be achieved and remember that what they want may not be what the participants want. This is an important point, because if trainers know a long time in advance who is coming on the course, it is often wise to approach them beforehand with a preparation questionnaire to discover what they want from the event. In this way, trainers can match aims and objectives of training events to those of the participants – it is much more likely to be successful if participants and trainers start with similar objectives.

Sequence of material

There may only be one logical manner in which to present material and if this is the case, then trainers have little choice. However, there are many situations when the sequence can be varied, and it is useful to do this on occasions if the same course is being taught several times. By doing so it avoids some of the repetition that takes away some of the life of a good teaching and learning session. It might also be useful for the trainers to vary the sequence from that expected by the participants. For example, if trainers are teaching a new skill, it might be interesting to get the participants to simulate the procedure before teaching them, so that they know precisely what their needs are! Theory does not always precede practice!

It is also wise to start with the more simple and move to the more complex, or to start from what the participants already know and move to new material. It may also be useful to start with more instructor-led materials and move towards the more self-directed ones.

Trainers who lack confidence tend to stick to their prepared sequence, but if they are good and confident they should be prepared to depart from their script – especially when participants ask relevant and interesting questions. Always be prepared to 'go with the relevant question' but do not be waylaid, or preoccupied with one question or questioner.

Plan the introduction and conclusion

It is wise to plan the introduction and the conclusion separately. It is most off-putting to the participants if the opening of a session seems unprepared and not very direct. The old adage, 'If you don't strike oil in the first minute, stop boring!' is very true. Teachers and trainers should know precisely how they are going to open the session, how they are going to engage the participants and how they are going to know that they are pitching it at the right level. This is perhaps the most important few minutes in any session – it needs to be carefully thought out.

A similar argument can be made for the conclusion. Plan the route through the session which leads to a specific conclusion, or set of conclusions, but do not worry if the discussion with the participants deflects the sequence a little because that might have been more important than what was planned! There is a common fallacy about the conclusion, that is, the conclusion must nicely wrap up the whole session and the session leader brings the event to a gentle close. However, if this approach is used, then the leader is putting the participants' minds at rest and they may not continue to think about what has happened. It is useful, therefore, to think about the unanswered questions a session has raised and close with a question. In this way, the participants will go away thinking about the question, and the tutor has gained a little more time than that which was timetabled!

Teaching is a very skilled undertaking if it is to be done well, so this is one area where human resource specialists might look at further development for themselves. There are many courses in the education and training of adults available, some through distance learning, and it is very useful for staff developers to be experts in this area because, even when they are not teaching themselves, they can be evaluating external consultants whom they have hired to conduct specific training events for them.

However, if there is one other lesson to be remembered from this chapter it is this: We can never be over-prepared – but we are often under-prepared! We do need to know the material and be able to use it. In preparation, especially when dealing with unfamiliar situations, staff developers would be wise to write out everything in full and then summarize it, so that they have full notes of the material that they are going to teach. Having summaries means that the teacher can maintain eye contact while still performing and this is important for the learners and for the teacher. Teachers can be more sensitive to the group if they are looking at all the participants and if they are conscious of boredom, or a lack of understanding, they can adjust their material accordingly.

Presentation skills

Most staff developers will be required to make presentations at some time in their career. We list some of the factors which help to improve their presentation skills:

- Smile when you introduce yourself.
- Always face the audience.

- Look reasonably happy and smart.
- Project the voice without shouting – speak to the back of the room (perhaps pick a person and pitch the voice accordingly).
- Breathe correctly.
- Maintain eye contact with the audience gradually but look to different parts of the room.
- Aim to stimulate and motivate the audience – tell them the topic and how it is to be addressed, ie the structure of the talk.
- Rehearse your talk.
- Provide a well thought-out sequence of material – don't waste people's time.
- Evaluate learning material beforehand – use a good sequence of material, altering the teaching strategies regularly.
- Tell the audience about the timetable for the session, eg coffee break, lunch, practical session, etc and keep to it.
- Number notes on overhead transparencies beforehand in the order in which you will use them, then, if you drop them, it is relatively easy to put them back in order.
- Remain calm and relaxed – do not fidget or put your hands in your pockets.
- Do not turn your back on the audience, eg to read a screen.
- Speak clearly and concisely.
- Allow plenty of time for audience participation, discussions, etc.
- Ensure that everyone can see subject matter on the overheads.
- Have a few numbered 'prompt cards' to jog the memory (don't put much on them).
- Do not give too much information at any one time – most people have a limited optimum attention span.
- Keep the vocabulary to a level which will be understood by the audience.
- Involve the audience in discussions without making people feel embarrassed.
- Invite questions from time to time.
- Listen to what people have to say.
- Use plenty of visual aids, hand-outs, etc.
- Recap at the end.
- Ask a final question for people to think about.

Sometimes staff developers work as a team in presenting a training event. They should:

- decide well beforehand how the responsibilities will be shared
- work with other members of the team to discuss respective strengths and weaknesses in terms of organizing events, specialist knowledge and presentation of the event
- plan well ahead.

Methods in teaching and training

Staff developers should ensure that the methods they use in their courses are appropriate to the needs of participants. For example, a course on 'interpersonal skills' would probably include some role play. Most methods we have listed will be used by staff developers in the course of their work. In this section we shall discuss several of the most widely used methods where the staff developer acts as trainer and facilitator in training events. Only a few methods are used most of the time in training sessions, eg straight lecture-type sessions, small syndicate groups and demonstrations. Yet there are a very wide variety of methods that we can use – there are over 30! (see Jarvis, 1995). However, we need to be able to vary the menu of methods used in any one session in order to ensure that we get a continued interest in the topic – remember that many adults' attention span is no more than 15 to 20 minutes, and so we might want to vary the method occasionally, or at least distract the participants' attention with a joke or something every so often, before re-engaging them in the task at hand.

Basically, the different methods of training are:

- trainer-led information or skills giving techniques (didactic)
- trainer-led information seeking methods (socratic)
- trainer-created, student-led methods (facilitative).

Examples of didactic methods tend to be based on providing a lecture, or a lecturette (short lecture), or a demonstration, followed by discussion. Socratic methods tend to involve questioning techniques, thus eliciting information. Facilitative methods include discussion-based approaches, projects or self-directed assignments, etc. Some of these methods are contained in the following list:

Teacher-centred methods

- controlled discussion
- demonstration
- guided discussion
- lecture
- lecture discussion
- mentoring
- tutorial.

Student-centred group methods

- brainstorming
- buzz groups

- case study
- debate
- fishbowl
- group discussion
- interview
- listening and observing
- panel (of experts)
- project
- role play
- simulation and games
- snowballing (methods of discussing a problem)
- 'T' groups (therapy groups)
- visits, tours and field trips
- workshops.

Individual student-centred methods

- assignments
- computer-assisted learning
- personalized systems of instruction
- personal tutorial
- practicals
- projects.

There are some basic rules to all the methods but we cannot expound them all here so we will examine some of the most popular ones. Remember, in all teaching methods, the aim is to help the participants learn, to feel part of the process and, where appropriate, be an active participant in the learning. Learning is a co-operative, not a competitive, venture. Education and training should be humanistic and moral and participants should never feel put down or afraid of contributing. Therefore, always put them at their ease and ensure that shy people are drawn into the group.

Lectures and presentations

Lectures and presentations are relatively easy to set up and a skilled lecturer can inspire and motivate, but a poor one can kill a topic stone dead. Remember the old adage – 'I tell them what I'm going to tell them, then I tell them, then I tell them what I've told them.' This is a wise psychology for lecturing.

Brainstorming

Brainstorming is an approach where a group, usually relatively small, seeks to solve a real or simulated problem by suggesting solutions, however likely or unlikely, which are collected during a specified period of time, often within a few hours. During the period when suggestions are being made, no discussion is allowed about any suggestion. This approach promotes creativity and is often enjoyable. This is used with small groups of up to 10 people to stimulate thought, eg for serious problem-solving. Here's how to brainstorm:

- Present a group of participants with a real or simulated problem.
- Ask them to put forward ideas to solve it, however outlandish.
- Collect all ideas from the group, but not in any special sequence.
- List them on a flip chart or ask one of the group to do it.
- Do not attempt to be judgmental.
- Allow enough time – some ideas will come quickly within a few minutes, others after a pause.
- Later discuss the ideas – the one preferred by the group is put forward as a solution to the problem.
- Discuss implementation of the 'solution'.
- Stop the discussion and summarize the results within the allotted time.

Buzz group

This is used for discussions and problem-solving – a small group of two or three people are asked to stop and consider something for a very short period of time, usually less than five minutes, and then raise questions, suggest solutions, priorities etc.

Discussion group

There are times when group discussion appears to participants as an excuse for less preparation, but if they are to work well they need careful planning. However, it is wise not to overdo their use. They are advantageous when used well and they do encourage wide participation:

- Keep the groups relatively small (six to eight people), so that everybody can participate.
- Choose the topic carefully and precisely.
- Ensure that different groups know if they are discussing the same or different topics.
- Make sure that the group has a chairperson, or elects one. If possible, tell the groups what the role of the chairperson will be, and that they will be expected to encourage everybody to participate, etc and to complete the task in the allocated time.
- If there is to be feedback, make sure that someone is prepared to provide it and knows how the feedback is to be presented, eg plenary discussion, written on blackboard or flip chart.

- Keep careful watch over the groups and make sure that most members are participating. If someone is dominating, try to make sure that others are encouraged to speak.
- Ensure that everybody knows the time they have to work together.
- Give the groups warning when they are reaching the end of their specified period.
- Try not to bring the discussion to a close when everybody is talking and the level of discussion is high – wait for a relatively quiet moment, if possible.
- Have the feedback mechanism carefully planned.

Role play

Role play helps participants to understand the importance of understanding different viewpoints. They each take on given roles and act out real-life situations, sometimes involving conflict or aggression. The scenarios for successful role play have to be prepared very carefully indeed. If they have not been precisely prepared, the whole session can easily go badly wrong. Usually the role players improvise and respond spontaneously to each other while also learning from their interaction. Ensure that the role play situation:

- is as close to reality as is feasible
- is not too stressful
- does not get out of hand.

Debrief participants after sessions so that they do not continue their roles once the exercise is over. A frequent fault in role play sessions is not to allow sufficient time for debriefing. Allow longer than the role play itself and, if the role play involved any form of stress, then the debriefing has to be even longer.

Many people do not like role play situations and no trainer should lead such a session unless he or she participates, or is prepared to participate, in the session. Often this is best done by the staff developer acting out a scenario in front of the whole group first.

Case studies

The use of projects and case studies help problem-solving techniques:

- The case needs to be researched well beforehand by the staff developer.
- It must be a realistic situation.
- It may involve problem-solving.
- Ask participants to study the situation.
- Devise a solution and illustrate how it might be implemented, etc.

- Allow discussion or interaction in order to share the responses at the end – but not always through a traditional plenary session – try to find some more imaginative approaches, like poster presentations.

Use of information technology in learning

Computer-assisted learning (CAL) is useful because it allows participants to work at their own pace. However, setting up a computer-based classroom may be an expensive undertaking in the first instance. At the same time, computer-based teaching does not have to occur in the classroom of the training department. Problems with CAL are that:

- it may create a real-time, real-life situation but it can be expensive in terms of the time and resources needed
- the simulation can be stressful, so reassure the psychological well-being of participants
- participants need to be familiar with computers.

In the next chapter we shall discuss the use of audio-visual aids. Evaluation· is discussed in Chapter 17.

Staff developers should:

- know their material

- be aware of the different learning styles of trainees

- prepare well

- become experts in the variety of methods used to teach and use them

- remain aware that good sequencing of material is important

- aim to have excellent presentation skills.

References and Further Reading

Buckley, R and Caple, T (1991) *One-to-one Training and Coaching Skills*, Kogan Page, London.

Clarke, D (1988) *Organising and Running Training Events*, National Extension College, Cambridge.

Corder, C (1990) *Teaching Hard, Teaching Soft*, Gower, Aldershot.

Ellington, H and Race, P (1993) *Producing Teaching Materials*, (2nd edn), Kogan Page, London.

Field, L and Drysdale, P (1991) *Training for Competence*, Kogan Page, London.

Guliano, D (1984) Instructing, in Nadler, L (ed.), *The Handbook of Human Resource Development*, John Wiley, New York, pp.8.1–8.20.

Honey, P and Mumford, A (1986) *Manual of Learning Styles*, Peter Honey, Maidenhead.

Jaques, D (1991) *Learning in Groups*, Kogan Page, London.

Jarvis, P (1995) *Adult and Continuing Education Theory and Practice*, (2nd edn), Routledge, London.

Jarvis, P (1997) *Ethics and the Education of Adults in Late Modern Society*, NIACE, Leicester.

Malasky, EW (1984) Instructional Strategies: Nonmedia, in Nadler, L (ed.), *Handbook of Human Resource Development*, John Wiley, New York, pp.9.1–9.8.

Pepper, AD (1992) *Managing the Training and Development Function*, (2nd edn), Gower, Aldershot.

Rogers, J (1989) *Adults Learning*, (3rd edn) Open University Press, Milton Keynes.

Stuart, C (1988) *Effective Speaking*, Gower, Aldershot.

Chapter 16

Using audio-visual aids

As information technology is developing so rapidly, so the use of audio-visual aids is becoming a much more specialist process. Once upon a time, it was the blackboard and chalk but now it can be audio, computer program, video, film, CD ROM, etc. Now there are catalogues of materials, and staff developers should endeavour to obtain some of them and build up small libraries of relevant material.

As all the new aids emerge, there is a tendency to concentrate on the new and omit the old. However, the old still have very important roles to play. For instance, using the chalkboard to produce a diagram to draw out the salient points of a complex theory is still as useful as a nicely produced video – and a lot cheaper!

Like teaching methods, there are a vast number of different audio-visual materials, and Ellington and Race (1993) divide these into seven types:

- printed and duplicated materials
- non-projected display materials
- still projected display materials
- audio materials
- linked audio and still visual materials
- video material
- computer-mediated materials.

Printed and duplicated materials

- hand-outs
- assignment sheets
- individualized study materials
- resource materials for group exercises.

Non-projected display materials

- chalkboard displays
- markerboard displays
- feltboard displays
- hook-and-loop board displays
- magnetic board displays
- flip chart displays
- charts and wallcharts
- photographic prints
- mobiles
- models
- dioramas
- realia.

Still projected display materials

- overhead projector transparencies
- slides
- filmstrips
- microfilm.

Audio materials

- radio broadcasts
- audio discs
- audiotapes.

Linked audio and still visual materials

- tape–slide programmes
- tape–photograph programmes
- filmstrips with sound
- radio–vision programmes
- tape–text
- tape model, tape realia, etc.

Video material

- tape film programmes
- television broadcasts
- videotape records
- videodisc recordings.

Computer-mediated materials

- number-crunching and data processing packages
- 'substitute tutor' packages
- 'substitute laboratory' packages
- database systems
- computer-managed learning systems
- interactive video system
- multimedia interactive systems.

It is important that a good training department is well equipped and staff developers should get catalogues from the producers of audio-visual equipment. They should ensure that there is a budget for such and purchase relevant equipment for the department, eg projectors, white boards, multimedia computers, etc. Equipment also needs professional maintenance – keep a careful record of when various pieces of equipment were serviced and when they next need servicing. Flip charts are very useful at meetings and many other activities within an organization and it saves time to buy several for distribution to departments where they are used most often.

An example of one of the most useful recent pieces of equipment that has been introduced has been the white board that produces photocopies of what has been written on it. Often students try very hard to reproduce a teacher's diagram – now it becomes possible. Large visual display units are also useful when using computers for demonstrations. It is these advances in ordinary equipment that demonstrate the training department's professionalism.

When preparing a session, staff developers have to decide what audio-visual aids they are going to use and prepare them carefully. In large organizations, there may be specialist assistants who make overhead transparencies or help with the use of specialist technical equipment. If this is not available, then staff developers should familiarize themselves with one of the computer programs, such as PowerPoint, that will help produce visual aids to a high standard. One of the things people remember clearly is the audio-visuals, and so staff developers should recognize that the professionalism of the department will be remembered through the use or lack of these media.

Teachers should always familiarize themselves with the equipment prior to conducting the session and know that their programme works by previewing it. Always know where there are replacements, such as bulbs, so that emergencies can be coped with in a professional manner.

Using audio-visual projected material

- Arrange seating so that everyone can see the display screen(s). Several different seating plans are given in Figure 16.1. Screens should be placed at a suitable distance from the projector.

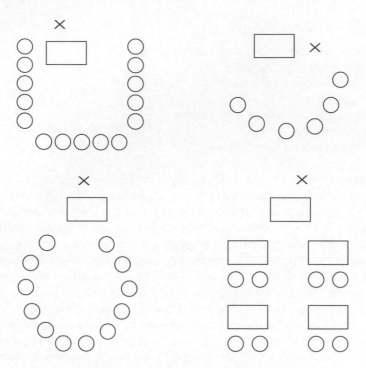

Figure 16.1   *Several seating plans for audio-visual material*
           Key: x = projector; rectangle = table; circle = seat

- Set up videos, projectors, etc beforehand so that they work at the touch of a switch.
- Make sure there are several monitors if there is a large audience.
- Keep spare projector bulbs handy.
- Keep an alternative source of material in case of a power failure or breakdown of equipment.
- Remember that if audio-visual material is being used, a teaching room that can be darkened is a necessity.
- Write clearly or use typed or word-processed material wherever possible.
- Do not put too much writing on overheads, eg not much more than two or three lines of writing.
- Number and name overheads.
- Use colour to emphasize points on overheads.
- Make sure that films and videos are of good quality and contain relevant subject matter.
- Only use flip charts, white boards or blackboards for small groups of people, eg less than 30.
- Put slides into slide projectors in the correct order. It is worth running through the whole set beforehand to ensure that they do not appear upside down.

- Ensure that all the equipment is there early on the day of the event – it is surprising what goes missing just when it is needed. Make sure it is secure when you are not using it.
- It helps if writing material is provided for taking notes.

Rooms should be prepared before the training event begins. Caretakers usually put desks and chairs in rows and if the trainer wants different arrangements, these should be specified beforehand, if possible.

It is essential to recognize that one of the most important jobs in teaching and training is furniture removing – ensuring that the room is ready for the training event.

Hand-outs

People like to take something away from the course or workshop that they have attended. Consequently, ensure that there are hand-outs from as many sessions as possible. They should be well produced for a specific purpose and not merely produced for the sake of the participants having something in their hands. If applicable, use pictures and diagrams to make them more interesting. If the text is too long, people are unlikely to read it all. Hand-outs should be included in the introductory folder about the course, unless the trainer does not wish them to be seen until after an exercise or a session has been completed. Ensure that if hand-outs are in colour they will photocopy clearly. It may be better to provide black and white patterns for graphs which reproduce well.

Contingency plans

An important task is to preview learning material such as video-based training tapes to ensure that they are of good quality. Always have a back-up plan in the event of the unforeseen happening:

- Always have spare teaching material for use in the event of power or equipment failure.
- Carry an alternative video tape, film or slides to use if others are lost or damaged.

It is not possible to be over-prepared in this respect. One of the problems with this is that the amount of preparation never shows until things go wrong! Then everybody becomes aware of the lack of preparation. Consequently, participants should not necessarily know how much preparation has gone into the event.

In Chapter 17 we shall discuss ways of evaluating training events.

Staff developers should:

- keep up-to-date with information about new audio-visual material
- understand how the various pieces of equipment operate
- attend audio-video roadshows so as to investigate new training materials
- make contingency plan for events
- always be very thorough checking all the equipment and having it serviced professionally
- check the teaching rooms and their layout before sessions begin.

References and Further Reading

Corder, C (1990) *Teaching Hard, Teaching Soft*, Gower, Aldershot.
Ellington, H and Race, P (1993) *Producing Teaching Materials*, (2nd edn), Kogan Page, London.
Field, L and Drysdale D (1991) *Training for Competence*, Kogan Page, London.
Laird, D (1985) *Approaches to Training and Development*, (2nd edn), Addison-Wesley, Reading, Mass.
Robinson, KR (1988) *A Handbook of Training Management*, (2nd edn), Kogan Page, London.

Chapter 17

Evaluating training events

In today's world, the quality of the product has become paramount in many people's minds. Most organizations that sponsor education and training initiatives quite reasonably expect that these programmes should be cost-effective in terms of learning by individuals, and the subsequent transfer of skills, knowledge and attitudes to a given job or task. Trainers and educators are, therefore, not exempt from this process and so we will look briefly at evaluation here. Put simply, evaluation is putting a value on a product or a process and while many techniques used in evaluation appear to give it a 'scientific' objectivity, it is an appearance rather than an empirical fact because values have no empiricism in them whatsoever. Evaluation is always qualitative and never quantitative, although it is possible to collect numbers of qualitative data in order to give the appearance of quantitative data. Numbers have a value but it is only to the person who wants statistical returns.

This chapter looks at three main things – why evaluate, what to evaluate and how to evaluate, and offers a discussion about evaluating the whole training function of the organization. It concludes by discussing what training departments should do with the evaluations they have collected.

Why evaluate?

There are a number of reasons why it is important to undertake evaluation. Some of them are included below but this is by no means an exhaustive list. It is essential to:

- know whether the course or session met the objectives of the participants
- know whether the processes of the course were satisfactory
- find out what course participants thought about all speakers or demonstrators

- know whether the content was relevant
- discover how much the participants have learned
- discover the impact, where applicable, of the course on the organization or department
- have data that can be used in preparing and marketing future training
- know what can be used again
- gain the support of managers or other sponsors
- try to estimate the cost-effectiveness of the training event.

It is important for staff developers to know precisely why they are evaluating the courses and workshops that they have run since it is impossible to plan an evaluation strategy otherwise. At the same time, it is important to recognize that if the training department mindlessly follows all the evaluation comments received, it would be 'swayed by every wind of doctrine' and every wish and whim of the participants. It is possible for the trainer to have a bad day or to have misunderstood the information and this may reflect the training department rather than the trainer, etc. Evaluation, therefore, is a complex but very important process.

What to evaluate

There are also a number of things that may be evaluated, such as:

- the learning processes
- the teaching processes
- audio-visual aids
- content
- the product
- the premises and location
- accommodation or meals where residential training has been conducted
- long-term outcome in terms of transference of skills to the workplace
- cost-effectiveness.

When training is external, then the training department should still evaluate the course and it might be wise to have a specially prepared schedule of questions to ask all employees who attend an external course. This could include a report about the course and its relevance. It is necessary for training departments to know about the quality of other providers.

Tutors and trainers might be more interested in some ways in the process and the content, but knowing the product (what has been learned) and the impact – what was the result of the training – is important to the line managers. As we saw in Chapter 10, there are, however, a few problems about reporting back to line managers on training sessions since the participants might not wish the trainer to provide their line manager with some of the confidential information so often discussed during a course. Moreover, they would not necessarily share all their other learning aspirations with the staff developer. Hence, the extent to which there is feedback has to be very carefully considered and confidentiality maintained about sensitive issues. At the same time, trainees should be encouraged to feed back their evaluations to their line managers, so that the training department can receive another form of evaluation – through the line managers.

Many people might want to know about the cost-effectiveness of a training event. Full costs should always be included in working these out; the following list might prove useful:

- salaries of participants including full economic costs such as pension contributions
- salaries of in-house staff developers or other in-house trainers
- fees for external tutors, trainers or consultants
- costs for training accommodation and services, eg heating and cleaning
- costs of external courses
- hotel accommodation
- travel and subsistence fees for staff participating in external courses
- costs of resources such as training computers, simulators, video machines and tapes, specialized equipment, overhead projectors, etc
- general costs incurred by the training department.

Indirect costs due to a reduction in staff output (which may occur as a result of staff participating in courses) are not usually included.

It might prove surprising to discover how much of the company budget does go on training. In France, America and the United Kingdom, companies may spend between 1 and 2 per cent of their budget on training.

Evaluation reports may also be very important for advertising future training sessions but they should be used selectively in this and without necessarily pointing to the person who was previously trained on the course.

How to evaluate

Evaluation is a form of research and should be treated in that way, although it is often hastily prepared just before, or during, the actual training event. It is wise to plan in advance the types of evaluation that are going to be employed, so that the tutor can tell the line managers when they are advertising the training event. If the line managers are paying something towards the course, then they want to know how their money is being spent and what return they are getting. Hence, having planned the evaluation, it becomes a useful tool in marketing the course.

There are a number of ways to evaluate and some of the methods are:

- formal or informal interviews
- end of event formal evaluation session
- use of questionnaires – at the end of a course and completed before leaving
- questionnaires sent to participants when they return to their workplace and again six months later (impact evaluation). The response rate to a questionnaire is approximately 40–50 per cent although if they are warned that they will be asked to complete one and that it is expected by management as well as the training department, the response rate might be higher
- estimates of the numbers of staff who participated in programmes and the drop-out rates for longer events
- number of requests to attend other events
- feedback from line managers
- improvement in work-based skills, knowledge or attitudes
- quality of products
- academic or practical standards reached
- formal certification
- a cost-benefit analysis.

Evaluation can be formative, summative and impact. These types may be conducted in the following ways:

- Formative evaluation, eg by discussion or interview. This is useful early on in a course to get the participants' feedback on the course up until that time. This can be either formal or informal.
- Summative evaluation – end-of-session questionnaires or interviews.
- Impact evaluation – after the session or course has finished (impact) – this can be with the participants, their colleagues or their line managers and it can be by interview or questionnaire. Asking colleagues may be dangerous and perhaps not very moral, so that they should be approached only after the trainee has suggested it.

Outcomes of competency-based or academic learning may also be assessed on the standard of learning achieved, eg qualifications awarded from a variety of awarding bodies. These may include National Vocational Qualifications, university degrees or diplomas, certificates of competence from professional societies and associations. Most will require external assessment which can be organized via the training department.

Remember that preparing a questionnaire is a very skilled business. Frequently, evaluation questionnaires are poorly designed and not worth the paper on which they are printed. Often low response rates are due to poorly designed questionnaires; indeed, the authors of this book will not in principle reply to a badly designed questionnaire, adopting the attitude that if the questioner could not be bothered to prepare it properly, why should anybody be prepared to spend precious time answering it?

Before preparing a questionnaire, do consult a good book about designing questionnaires and other evaluation instruments. There are one or two recommended in the references. We considered giving examples of questionnaires here but rejected it because each training event is designed for a specific reason and so questionnaires need to be quite specific in their design. That does not mean to say that when good questions have been prepared they should not be included in many different questionnaires Indeed, this is how questionnaire design can get easier but it comes with a lot of practice and rigorous analysis. If there are a number of staff in the training department, it is always wise to test out the evaluation questionnaire on a colleague before it is printed to make sure that it is asking for precisely the information that the department needs, and no more!

Formal and informal training initiatives can be evaluated in other ways. Staff developers can do the following:

- Wander into offices and talk to people, if they are not too busy. It takes only a few minutes for staff to tell an evaluator if they have learned from a training initiative. If they are very pleased or very angry about a particular initiative or event, many of them will soon say so!
- Arrange to meet line managers to discuss their views – either from their own experience of the training function or how they view the progress of their staff.
- Discuss with staff who undertake practical skills, whether they can perform tasks better following training.
- Meet a cross-section of suppliers or customers of the organization to obtain information on how they view staff attitudes and competence.
- Evaluate tutors' input to in-house courses from the point of view of participants.
- Sit in at sessions conducted by others as a matter of course.
- Assess attendance at seminars, eg do staff regularly go to them and consider them worth attending?
- Obtain the view of the Personnel Department about the aspects that concern them, such as health and safety.

Offering feedback after a learning event

Sometimes, staff developers might be asked by staff whom they have sent on a training event, or by visiting consultants, for feedback. This is more likely if they know that the training department conducts evaluations of all the events. But staff developers might also wish to provide feedback after a training event.

Feedback is very useful to teachers, trainers and learners even if it is not always complimentary. Remember these few useful points when providing it:

- Choose the right time and place.
- Try to prepare the main points that are to be communicated.
- Look for positives as well as negatives in someone's work or behaviour.
- Be specific about what was liked or disliked – share ideas or information rather than just giving advice.
- Be sincere.
- Look at the person.
- Remain non-judgmental – focus feedback on the behaviour rather than on the person.
- Do not criticize.
- Ensure that the person receiving the feedback feels helped by what is said.
- Be prepared to receive feedback yourself in a pleasant manner.

Some organizations merely send a summary of the points made as a result of the evaluation. This is rather impersonal, and not the best method of maintaining good contact and support with the people who are going to act as trainers and consultants for the company. Always try to be personal in this matter, especially when the feedback is difficult to provide.

Evaluating the overall training function

Periodically, it is worthwhile for the training department to conduct a review of its own activities. It is worth making a formal approach to department heads to see whether they feel that the training department is successfully undertaking what they want from it and what more it might do. It is also important to get them to say something about the department's own attitude, the resources it makes available to employees, etc. In addition, it is worth looking at both organizational growth and health and safety.

Organizational growth and development

In some instances, increased training may be easily measured in terms of increased productivity, eg by workers on a production line. In other instances, eg management training, the benefits to the organization or its staff may not be recognized until long after the training event.

Health and safety

There are many examples of where training can increase safety within the workplace and there is often a legal requirement for certain aspects of safety training that must be enforced by the staff developer. Moreover, staff developers and other interest groups may feel that union or employee pressure for training fully justifies the expense in terms of time and other resources in that it makes for good working relationships. Evaluators must expect to get a wide range of opinions from staff as every person's perceptions of quality in training are variable, depending on the standards to which they aspire. Opinions of the line manager on perceived increases or decreases in productivity, health, safety, efficiency and effectiveness of the whole organization have to be taken into account.

Self-evaluation

There is also a place for self-evaluation of the overall training processes, the equipment, the costs and the usefulness to the organization and to individual employees. Remember, however, that no empirical cost can provide a factual statement of the worth of training! There can be normative and comparative evaluations – both are useful.

Self-evaluations have to be brutally honest to be worthwhile! Often others are kinder!

Using the evaluation data

There are a variety of uses for the data collected from evaluations. Staff developers can begin to get an overall picture of:

- all aspects of the training programme
- the extent to which staff training needs are being met
- line managers' reaction to courses
- the extent to which the programme is effective in the organization
- the ability of all the trainers, lecturers and demonstrators
- external providers and the level of their courses
- the cost-effectiveness of the training
- the ancillaries of the programme, eg accommodation, food, facilities.

Staff developers should not be swayed by a single bad evaluation, but if a picture emerges over two or three events, then they should act either to replace or alter that which is being criticized or try to introduce some training and development for the teacher being criticized – if that falls within the remit of the training department.

However, the data obtained should be collated into the training department's report. This report should be distributed not only to the management but to all members of staff. The report can become an important instrument in generating a training culture in the organization. It should contain information on:

- types of course made available throughout the year
- numbers of staff who participated in given courses (data for external and internal courses can be shown separately)
- number of competencies, certificates, diplomas, degrees, etc gained throughout the year
- whether people found the learning useful
- whether line managers felt that their staff had been able to transfer their learning to the workplace.

As well as the evaluative data, the report might contain items of news about new developments in training that are occurring elsewhere, so that managers are aware of these new initiatives.

Specific data may be useful when the staff developer is called upon to provide information to senior management about policy matters. Indeed, the more information about training developments that the training department is able to provide, the more significant the place of training is likely to be.

Staff developers should:

- evaluate all aspects of staff development – learn all the techniques of evaluation

- regard much of the informal work of the staff developer as evaluative

- seek to improve the training

- make the training department even more professional

- prepare evaluation reports for directors and all members of the company

- indicate new developments in training.

References and Further Reading

Bramley, P (1986) *Evaluation of Training: A Practical Guide,* British Association for Commercial and Industrial Education, London.

Burton, C, Grandi, E, Martin, K and Hallmark, A (1987) The experience transfer learning process, *Training and Development,* 6(7): 45–9.

Field, L and Drysdale, D (1991) *Training for Competence,* Kogan Page, London.

Fletcher, S (1992) *NVQs: Standards and Competence,* (2nd edn), Kogan Page, London.

Goldstein, IL (1986) *Training in Organizations: Needs Assessment, Development and Evaluation,* (2nd edn), Brooks/Cole Publishing, Pacific Grove, CA.

Guba, E and Lincoln, Y (1981) *Effective Evaluation,* Jossey-Bass, San Francisco and London.

Industrial Society Information Dept (1985) *Survey of Training Costs*, New Series no. 1, The Industrial Society, London.

Kirkpatrick, DL (1998) *Evaluating Training Programs: The Four Levels*, Berrett-Koehler, San Francisco.

Robinson, DG and Robinson, JC (1989) *Training for Impact: How to Link Training to Business Needs and Measure the Results*, Jossey-Bass, San Francisco.

Sanderson, G (1992) Objectives and evaluation, In Truelove, S (ed.), *Handbook of Training and Development*, Blackwell, Oxford, pp.114–71.

PART 4

Occupation of HRD professionals

Chapter 18

Training-related organizations

A major task for staff developers is to establish and maintain contact with a wide variety of organizations such as local Training and Enterprise Councils, career services, schools, universities and colleges or commercial and government organizations. They also need to network with other staff developers and consultants. In this chapter we provide information about some of the organizations which are involved in sponsoring training programmes of various kinds. We have provided a list of useful addresses in Appendix B.

National training schemes

Staff developers must be aware of national and international education and training initiatives. For example, they should be aware of local schemes to help redundant or other unemployed individuals. In a similar manner, there are community education schemes, which are available to a wide range of groups whether in work, leisure or unemployed. Various initiatives are sponsored by the Department for Education and Employment (DfEE) in the UK, mainly through local Training and Enterprise Councils (TECs) or Local Enterprise Councils (LECs). There are also local government-sponsored job centres in most large towns. The NVQ and GNVQ competency-based scheme, which is sponsored by the Qualification and Curriculum Authority, represents useful opportunities for staff in organizations and also for the unemployed.

Training and Enterprise Councils (TECs) and Local Enterprise Councils (LECs)

The numerous TECs and LECs throughout the UK provide a whole range of resources for staff developers and frequently offer subsidized courses. TECs act as regulators of the training market rather than providers of training. They have an overview of all local programmes that relate to vocational education and training. TECs are private companies formed by local business people who manage public investment in training programmes under contract to the government. They are in business to help organizations to invest in their staff and provide impartial help in a number of ways by acting as:

- advisors to analyse staff training needs, who will complete an action plan with staff developers or other representatives from the organization
- advisors to provide ongoing training support
- advisors of available training services
- providers of subsidized courses
- providers of grants towards the employment and training of previously long-term unemployed people
- providers of information about college and university courses
- providers of information about entrance requirements for particular courses
- advisors in career planning and development
- advisors about training loans for small firms.

Currently, TECs are also behind the scheme, 'Investors in People', (IIP) which offers sponsorship and subsidized courses to organizations that take a holistic approach to training staff, and this offers a wide range of training initiatives. Organizations which invest in IIP undertake to do the following:

- make a public commitment to develop all employees to achieve business objectives
- review the training and development needs of employees
- develop individuals and teams
- develop people throughout their employment, reviewing individual needs.

Enterprise Councils also sponsor the 'New Horizons' initiatives for young people (usually to be completed by the age of 25). These incorporate modern apprenticeships which guarantee on-the-job training and possibly day release. A modern apprenticeship lasts for approximately three years, depending on the subject matter and on the rate of progress of the trainee.

A related option is for young people to work and study towards National Vocational Qualifications (up to level 3 or above). This works in the following manner: the trainee and employer sign an agreement about the training to be provided, often a wage or allowance is paid during training and employers receive a contribution towards the training costs.

Some local TECs also provide information about Training Access Points (TAPs) which is a comprehensive database listing local training courses. TAP terminals are often available at local TECs, local libraries or career centres. This initiative includes a 'business' TAP team to provide training information for organizations. Several TECs also sponsor schemes whereby care is provided for school-age children while their parents are at work. The TEC National Council, in its response to the Government White Paper *Learning to Succeed* (1999), has welcomed the intention to develop greater cohesion between post-16 education and training, and the development of local Learning and Skills Councils from April 2001 to replace TECs.

National Vocational Qualifications (NVQs)

Competence-based National Vocational Qualifications (NVQs) and Scottish Vocational Qualifications (SVQs) are available at various levels (1–5). They describe the competencies expected of people in most occupations in the UK and indicate that holders of qualifications to the various levels attained are competent at their work. All NVQs and SVQs are delivered through a network of centres (which may include local colleges). These centres are approved by one of several awarding bodies, eg City and Guilds, which are accredited by the Qualifications Curriculum Authority and the Scottish Qualification Authority. Topics are divided into broad areas, and include the following:

- tending animals, plants and land
- extracting and providing natural resources
- constructing
- engineering
- manufacturing
- transporting
- providing goods and services
- providing health, social and protective services
- providing business services
- communicating
- developing and extending knowledge and skill.

The five NVQ levels provided as a general guide (see Qualifications and Curriculum Authority, 1997) are defined as shown.

Level 1

Competence which involves the application of knowledge in the performance of a range of varied work activities, most of which may be routine and predictable.

Level 2

Competence which involves the application of knowledge in a significant range of varied work activities, performed in a variety of contexts. Some of the activities are complex or non-routine, and there is some individual responsibility or autonomy. Collaboration with others, perhaps through membership of a work group or team, may often be a requirement.

Level 3

Competence which involves the application of knowledge in a broad range of varied work activities performed in a wide variety of contexts, most of which are complex and non-routine. There is considerable responsibility and autonomy, and control or guidance of others is often required.

Level 4

Competence which involves the application of knowledge in a broad range of complex, technical or professional work activities performed in a wide variety of contexts and with a substantial degree of personal responsibility and autonomy. Responsibility for the work of others and the allocation of resources is often present.

Level 5

Competence which involves the application of a significant range of fundamental principles across a wide and often unpredictable variety of contexts. Very substantial personal autonomy and often significant responsibility for the work of others and for the allocation of substantial resources feature strongly, as do personal accountabilities for analysis and diagnosis, design, planning, execution and evaluation.

Types of competency required to qualify for National Vocational Qualifications for Trainers are given in Appendix C. Staff developers can become assessors for NVQs if sufficiently well qualified. Many implement and monitor competency-based training for staff within their organization which may be undertaken with the help of local colleges or universities.

Assessment of vocational qualifications

The assessment of competence-based training towards National Vocational Qualifications (NVQs) represents a type of evaluation in that the standard reached by participants, following a period of training, is measured against national standards which, if reached, lead to certification. Guidance notes are available from the Qualifications and Curriculum Authority for those trainers involved in assessing and verifying NVQs.

Management Charter Initiative (MCI)

The MCI, set up in 1988, is the operating arm of the National Forum for Management Education and Development. It promotes best practice in management development, particularly competence-based initiatives for the benefits of organizations and their staff. The components of the Management Standards are divided up into seven key roles, each of which is subdivided into units. The various levels and number of units required for various categories of manager are given in Appendix D.

Liaising with local schools link officers

Sometimes staff developers work with schools link officers and university tutors mainly by organizing work experience for senior students. In this instance, staff developers must ensure that students are presented with work experience which should closely follow an authentic job and should ensure that they are supervised. It is usually best for the student to show the training staff a curriculum vitae and to attend for interview before the placement.

Local colleges and universities

Another important task of staff developers is to maintain contact with a wide variety of organizations such as universities and colleges, and government-run organizations. Local educational organizations are a valuable resource in terms of types and quality of staff development courses offered. They are well worth a frequent visit to discuss how the college or university can meet the training needs of the organization. Alternatively, since most of these organizations are client-oriented, they are usually pleased to send a representative to see line managers and staff developers in order to devise ways in which they can help. Many colleges and universities are also excellent sources of distance learning for adults of all ages and it is wise to remember that, in recent years, universities and colleges have become extremely flexible in the way that they provide courses. They often have courses that can be taken either by attending or by distance learning.

Commercial organizations that offer training

It is also useful to maintain contact with the representatives of training companies, of which there are many! Their brochures are a useful source of information. They provide information about:

- types of courses available and for whom
- standards to be achieved
- time needed to reach a given standard
- costs.

It is good to talk to other staff developers about commercial organizations, and to keep a record of reports from staff who have attended courses run by them, to see whether they provide good courses at a high standard and at reasonable costs.

Educational guidance and counselling

Staff developers are often expected to give advice about training and career development. Naturally, every experienced staff developer gains a great deal of knowledge in this field. However, there is also a national association on education and guidance and it is useful for staff developers to be aware of it, to be associated with it and receive its literature. Perhaps the best place to make contact with it is through the National Association of Educational Guidance for Adults (NAEGA). The more staff developers are able to make this resource available to staff, the more staff will come to the training department. It is always useful for staff developers to get to know the staff and their educational interests and needs.

Career counselling, however, is a little more specialized and staff developers have to be aware of the pitfalls in embarking upon this, especially if some of it is undertaken as a matter of course during annual appraisal meetings with line managers. For example, counselling is common for new recruits who may be unaware of career development opportunities. Staff developers might, however, have a record of local agencies that staff can approach if they need further advice. Once more, there is a national agency with which staff developers should be familiar, ie the Institute of Careers Guidance in Stourbridge. At the other end of the career spectrum, staff developers should be prepared to run pre-retirement courses for staff, or send them on courses run by other colleges and organizations. It is possible to buy in pre-retirement courses from specialists, such as The Pre-Retirement Association of Great Britain, in Guildford, Surrey (see Appendix B).

International contacts

There are several European initiatives of which staff developers need to remain aware. For example, the European Centre for the Development of Vocational Training (CEDEFOP) encourages the promotion and development of vocational training and in-service training within the European Union. Through its scientific and technical activities, it promotes various aspects of vocational training that include compilation of documentation and contributes to the co-ordination of research and development in vocational education. It also promotes exchange of information and experience on vocational education

The Leonardo da Vinci initiative is another European vocational programme that aims to improve initial and continuing vocational education. It provides support to a variety of projects in the field of vocational training. Another such project was 'Erasmus', which in 1992 had a £40 million budget with which to award grants for exchange visits by young participants in higher education. The scheme has now been replaced with another called 'Socrates'.

However, the important thing about all of these is that there are funds and schemes available from the European Union, and it is wise for staff developers to acquaint themselves with them. One of the best ways of making initial contact might be through local colleges and universities involved in such schemes.

Consultants

Most staff developers will find it useful to employ specialist trainers or consultants sometimes. Most are highly skilled and specialize in particular topics, eg Management Development, Team-Building. Beware of consultants who claim to specialize in almost everything – it takes considerable expertise and time to specialize in just one. Consultants can be expensive so make sure that they inform the training department exactly what they require in terms of fees, hotel allowances, travelling costs, etc.

Networking

It is always useful to communicate with other staff developers either in person, by telephone, by e-mail or by attending seminars and conferences. This way, staff developers will get to hear about new initiatives in training and development. If they have something new to say, they could arrange to give a paper at one of the annual HRD seminars. Such conferences are arranged by the Institute of Personnel and Development in London (see address in Appendix B). Many colleges and universities are now also organizing HRD conferences.

Training awards

There are several initiatives which encourage training departments to apply for an award. The local Training and Enterprise Council is a good source of advice about these.

Resource library

Staff developers have a wide range of support and guidance from many local and national organizations. However, it is not always possible to have all this information at their fingertips, so they should build up their own resource library in order to undertake the necessary research. This resource library should include:

- relevant publications about the industry
- EU and government documents
- trade union publications about training and development
- all local TEC publications
- reports about training initiatives in different companies, especially training initiatives undertaken by competitor organizations
- relevant lists of people who can be consulted: address, telephone, fax, e-mail and the World Wide Web
- brochures from colleges, universities and training companies
- brochures about CD ROM and other courses that can be purchased to be learned at a distance
- material from the BBC and other television companies
- basic books about training
- manuals of procedures, etc
- lists of Web sites
- lists of databases that hold information on training courses.

Staff developers should:

- communicate widely with local and national organizations

- inform managers and staff in their organization about initiatives which might provide them with advice or training

- maintain a resource library.

References and Further Reading

Blanchard, K and Spencer, J (1989) *The One-minute Manager*, Collins, Glasgow.
Churchill, P (1991) Training and Enterprise Councils, *Education and Training*, 33(3): 19–20.
Clegg, F (1982) *Simple Statistics: A Course Book for the Social Sciences*, Cambridge University Press, Cambridge.
Fletcher, S (1992) *NVQs: Standards and Competence*, (2nd edn), Kogan Page, London.
Jessup, G (1991) *Outcomes: NVQs and the Emerging Model of Education and Training*, Falmer, London.

Management Charter Initiative (1990) *Management Development in Action*, MCI, London.

NCVQ, *Data News*, Spring 97, 3, 5–6.

Woolfe, R, Murgatroyd, S and Rhys, S (1987) *Guidance and Counselling in Adult and Continuing Education: A Developmental Perspective*, Open University Press, Milton Keynes.

Chapter 19

The staff developer's own development

We have seen that staff developers have a commitment to helping staff in the organization to expand their skills. However, the staff developer's own development is something that must not be neglected in the course of helping others. In this chapter we shall examine some of many personal attributes and skills required by them, especially as they become more senior in larger departments and are required to manage other staff, and, finally, we shall look at qualification pathways for professionals.

Personal attributes needed by staff developers

The ability to cope with pressure is an essential attribute of staff developers and something for which they should be trained. Indeed, good personal relationships are essential. A recent survey of staff developers working for a research council in the United Kingdom showed that communication skills and good personal relationships are placed high on the list of attributes which they consider to be important. The lists of attributes discussed are shown:

- Be a good communicator.
- Build up good working relationships.
- Have good interpersonal skills.
- Be flexible.
- Be able to handle groups.
- Display confidence.
- Cope with pressure.
- Be proactive.

- Possess management skills.
- Possess personal credibility.
- Maintain a high profile.
- Have prestige within the organization.
- Think ahead.
- Remain articulate.
- Show initiative.
- Retain motivation.
- Remain enthusiastic.
- Possess an ability to solve problems.
- Have a lively personality.

This is an impressive list of attributes and there may be areas where staff developers need their own personal development, so it is always wise to look for courses that can assist in this development, but try to ensure that the amount of training undertaken by the training staff is similar to that expected by staff in other departments.

Intervention in staff development initiatives

Even where staff developers are not specialist interventionists, from time to time they may be called in to assist with some problem areas. For example, staff may have difficulty in getting enough time to participate in a course but line managers may feel that one or two of their staff are volunteering to attend courses so as to escape their normal working activities – thus a compromise has to be reached. Sometimes this means that a staff developer will need to intervene in disputes at individual level (most often between line managers and staff). In some instances there is a need to support staff, in others the line manager or project manager. When intervening, remember the following:

- there are always at least two sides to every dispute
- try to understand both points of view
- staff developers are there to help the organization and its staff improve their skills; what is the priority in this instance?

In order to be involved in these activities, staff developers should be aware of the types of skill necessary. They have to be assertive, but only within specific limits. Assertive behaviour often results in greater self-confidence but assertiveness does not mean that the wishes of others should not be respected. It means that if there is conflict, both sides can 'win' if they remain calm and confident. For example, a disagreement with another person can result in a working compromise so that both 'win'. It is good to be assertive but avoid appearing passive or too aggressive:

- Acknowledge the rights of the other person.
- Know the other's rights.
- Make time to think about what is to be said and if the time is inappropriate, say so, eg, 'Now is not the best time, let's discuss it later'.
- Remain aware that all decisions will affect future relationships.
- Remain sincere, relaxed and friendly.

Passive behaviour often results in:

- feeling uncomfortable
- feeling unhappy
- withdrawing from activities
- saying and doing nothing.

Examples of aggressive behaviour include:

- being angry
- dominating others
- remaining self-opinionated.

As far as possible, it is wise for the training department to maintain an 'open door' policy and this will be well received, so long as the staff developer is always seen to be a wise source of advice and guidance. Since the staff developer may be asked to intervene in such situations, it is wise for them to have the skills necessary, and so training in interpersonal skills may be an important, but often an overlooked area of personal development.

Management and leadership in training

Staff developers who assume a management position in the department need management and leadership skills. There are many books and courses on management and leadership so we are only pointing out the direction that senior staff need to move in.

Management styles may vary between being democratic and autocratic (see Guest, *et al.*, 1986). Democratic leaders provides plenty of freedom for colleagues while autocratic leaders assert their authority. In effect these styles represent the opposite ends of a continuum and most leadership styles fall somewhere in between. Leadership styles must take into account both the people being led and the situation.

Delegation

A good leader is able to delegate. It enables the team to improve productivity. It provides experience for staff and frees leaders to manage the more difficult areas:

- Explain to staff in person why delegation is important.
- Choose capable people who can manage the task within the time set.
- Remain open to criticism and accept that there may be other ways of performing tasks.
- Allow staff freedom to get the job done as they see best – provide training if they need it.

Chairing a formal meeting or discussion

Usually the leader controls and summarizes a discussion ensuring that it is run efficiently and with little time wasted:

- Having selected a topic, make sure that a meeting is really needed and for how long it is likely to last.
- Decide on the objectives.
- Decide what can be dealt with in the time available.
- Prepare a chart giving a heading for each aspect of the topic to be discussed (use a black or white board if preferred but here space is limited).
- Allow time for everyone who wishes to speak.
- Reach an agreed decision.

Leading a formal discussion

- Ask people to introduce themselves.
- Make sure everyone is comfortable.
- Introduce the topic and write it out for all to see.
- Proceed to discuss the first aspect of the topic – disclosing the first chart heading.
- Ensure that each member of the discussion group is encouraged to contribute.
- Listen carefully – staff developers should check on their understanding of what has been said.
- Summarize the contributions and write them down against the chart heading for all to see (ask questions and summarize – use open-ended questions).
- Repeat for all chart headings (add other chart headings if asked to do so by the group and discuss).
- Complete discussion about the topic.

- Once the discussion about the first topic has been exhausted, provide a final summary.
- Repeat the above procedure for other topics.

Careers of training professionals

As we have seen throughout this book, staff developers undertake a difficult and complex role. They bring their own personalities, values and attitudes and knowledge to their job. They need to have teaching and organization skills and also have to manage a complex role. They might be a very proactive 'change agent' working with management to solve organizational problems or developing the organization. On the other hand, they may prefer to act as 'providers' offering training designed to improve and maintain organizational performance rather than making great changes. As training managers, they may be concerned with the supervision and management of the whole training function which is undertaken mainly by staff junior to them.

Staff developers can often impose their own ideas onto the job. To a great extent each individual has to decide on the type of training job for which he or she would like to qualify. For example, a job involving large amounts of class contact time would best be undertaken by someone with good teaching experience and/or qualifications while a job requiring mainly negotiation, resource-gathering and delegation skills might require someone experienced in management techniques.

In practice, most staff developers remain up to date with technical and professional information and maintain an awareness of innovation in terms of learning techniques, new technology and other initiatives. So far as the type of job is concerned, staff developers have a wide variety of opportunities. Often the success of their job depends on their:

- aspirations
- knowledge
- experience
- formal qualifications
- personal skills
- energy
- level of proactivity
- level of commitment.

Throughout this book we have sought to present some ideas of the tasks and skills required for the work. Hence, staff developers have a great deal of freedom to design their own role but employers also have their own expectations of the role of staff developer. The following list provides a guide to what employers often require (Hargreaves, 1995):

- Change management.
- Facilitate change.
- Use political judgement.
- Develop philosophy.
- Formulate strategy.
- Create culture.
- Develop equal opportunity culture.
- Give input to HRD.
- Assess competencies.
- Diagnose.
- Liaise.
- Co-ordinate.
- Budget.
- Monitor.
- Manage personnel.
- Know COSHH regulations.
- Know appraisal systems.
- Understand methodology.
- Manage resources.
- Rotate jobs.
- Organize development.
- Recruit.
- Prioritize.
- Develop staff.
- Plan or organize training.
- Initiate development projects.
- Match means with supply.
- Know Management Charter Initiatives.
- Explore training possibilities.
- Develop students.
- Know employment law.
- Use open or distance learning.
- Know health and safety.
- Understand the principles of learning.
- Practise quality or TQM.
- Plan or design courses.
- Understand techniques.
- Prepare courses.
- Prepare visual aids.
- Produce distance learning packages.
- Organize seminars.
- Circulate course literature.
- Run workshops.
- Motivate or be motivated.

- Facilitate.
- Team-build.
- Coach.
- Train.
- Deliver or conduct courses.
- Monitor cost-effectiveness.
- Evaluate.
- Use information technology.
- Maintain records.
- Have business acumen.
- Employ customer care.
- Act as consultant.
- Advise.
- Counsel.
- Process NVQs.
- Undertake research.

As we have shown, some staff developers are specialists, others are generalists. Job titles may vary, ranging from 'Staff Developer' to 'Training Manager', 'Training Director' or 'Training Consultant'. Training professionals are expected to participate in a wide range of tasks including managing the training department, teaching staff and providing management development initiatives.

Keeping up to date

It is imperative to remain up to date with technical and professional information and to maintain an awareness of innovation in terms of learning techniques, new technology and other initiatives, knowledge of which could also be useful to managers and staff. It is also necessary to enhance communication and interpersonal skills and to build up good working relationships with interest groups, maintain awareness of new developments in training and staff development by attending seminars or conferences and by meeting with other staff developers to exchange ideas, successes or problems. There are several very successful ways for keeping up to date with innovation in staff development:

- Watch nationally televised programmes on the various methods used to promote learning and training.
- Read brochures and mail shots which advertise staff development courses. These are circulated routinely by government-sponsored and commercial organizations and provide a very useful source of information.
- Read journals designed for HR professionals. These are an effective source of information.
- Try to keep up with Web-based information.

Gaining experience

Staff developers should routinely monitor training methods to ensure that these remain acceptable to staff and that a reasonably high proportion of learning is achieved by participants in courses. They should remain up to date with new technology and computer software. So as to improve professional practice, it is often beneficial to do the following:

- Sit in on staff development initiatives as an observer so as to obtain insight into the variety of processes involved in training.
- Meet other staff developers at training-related seminars.
- Serve on a general committee within your organization – so long as it is not too time-consuming.
- Participate in a high profile course for trainers – you might meet an excellent role model.
- Develop your organization skills as a voluntary member of a committee in your spare time.
- Network with other staff developers to give you an insight into the various types of work available.

Skills in information technology

Learn to use computer graphics. There are several excellent software packages which will help to set up a training database and also produce creative and well-formatted, clear, professional-looking documents. If you are not skilled in undertaking all forms of writing and designing it is worth attending a course on the subject. Learn to use databases for storing and retrieving training-related information.

Appraisal

Remember that your line manager or director will be appraising you – find out precisely how your work is viewed. Improve on it.

Qualification pathways

Experience counts for much and currently staff developers can choose whether they wish to obtain formal qualifications or not. On the other hand, some employers may require formal qualifications, particularly for high-level jobs. Qualifications may be gained in several ways, eg via:

- an NVQ/GNVQ/SVQ programme of learning
- a series of short formal courses
- successful completion of a full-time or part-time degree-level or post-graduate-level course.

Information about career pathways and qualifications for staff developers may be obtained from the Institute for Personnel and Development (IPD) in London.

National Vocational Qualifications

A network of National Training Organisations (NTOs) have been set up by the Department of Education and Employment in the UK. NTOs have a responsibility for developing national occupational standards, and act as gatekeepers to the vocational qualification movement, eg NVQs and GNVQs. These competence-based initiatives are delivered through a network of centres approved by one of several awarding bodies eg City & Guilds or EdExcel. Qualifications which may be gained include the following:

- NVQ and SVQ Level 3 in Training and Development (for those involved in training individuals or groups, ie the identification of training needs, design and delivery of sessions, reviewing and evaluating the outcome)
- NVQ and SVQ Level 4 Human Resource Development
- NVQ and SVQ Level 4 in Learning Development
- NVQ and SVQ Level 5 in Training and Development Strategy.

The level of entry depends on previous experience. (Please see Appendix C.)

Commercially run courses

Short courses

There are numerous short courses for staff developers ranging from one-day courses to one-week courses. These include a wide range of topics including training techniques and presentation. Topics on 'Health and Safety' especially for those involved in presenting such subjects may also be offered.

Longer courses

IPD sponsor courses for entrants into training practice. This includes a Certificate in Training Practice (CTP) which involves at least 120 hours of study. Topics include: identification of training needs, training design, delivery and evaluation of training. It may be studied at some regional centres.

Open learning and distance learning courses

These are run by a number of organizations including the University of Surrey. Open learning allows access by the majority of people regardless of age or qualifications. Emphasis is on flexibility in the approach of learners and trainers. Programmes are often modular in design, each module comprising a discrete, substantial, free-standing unit of information. Often modules are arranged in sets and can be 'mixed and matched' depending on the needs of the individual.

Degree courses

Full-time and part-time postgraduate degree courses with Training or Staff Development or Change Agent Skills as a main topic are provided by the University of Leicester and the University of Surrey.

Accreditation

Whatever qualification you hold, it is best to write to the Institute of Personnel and Development (IPD, see address in Appendix B) which can advise you on accreditation. 'Achievement of Professional Standards' accepted by IPD may include:

- syllabus-based educational programmes
- NVQs and SVQs
- portfolio of experience plus assessment
- assessment of prior certificated learning eg graduate or postgraduate qualifications.

Staff developers should:

- update their skills regularly

- develop their careers

- network with other people

- remain up to date with procedures for obtaining qualifications, eg NVQs, day-release courses.

References and Further Reading

Adair, J (1983) *Training for Leadership*, Gower Publishing, Aldershot.

Employment Occupational Standards Council (1995) *Training and Development Standards Guidance on Possible Use of Evidence across Units*, Department for Education and Employment, London.

Employment Occupational Standards Council (1996) *Training and Development Qualifications Structure*, Department for Education and Employment, London.

Field, L and Drysdale, D (1991) *Training for Competence*, Kogan Page, London.

Fletcher, S (1992) *NVQs: Standards and Competence*, (2nd edn), Kogan Page, London.

Guest, RH, Hersey, P and Blanchard, KH (1986) *Organisational Change through Effective Leadership*, (2nd edn), Prentice-Hall, Englewood Cliffs, New Jersey.

Gutteridge, TG (1986) Organizational career development systems: the state of the practice, in Hall, DT and Associates (eds), *Career Development in Organisations*, Jossey-Bass, San Francisco, pp.50–94.

Hall, DT (1986) Breaking career routines: mid-career choice and identity development, in Hall, DT and Associates (eds), *Career Development in Organisations*, Jossey-Bass, San Francisco, pp.120–159.

Hargreaves, PM (1995) *The Training Officer: A Cost-effective Role in a Science Research Organisation?*, unpublished PhD thesis, University of Surrey.

Honey, P (1988) *Face-to-Face: A Practical Guide to Interactive Skills*, Gower, Aldershot.

Institute of Personnel and Development (1997), *Qualification Routes*, IPD, London.

London, M (1988) *Change Agents*, Jossey-Bass, San Francisco.

Management Charter Initiative (1990) *Management Development in Action*, Management Charter Initiative, London.

Scott, B (1986) *The Skills of Communicating*, Gower, Aldershot.

The National Training Organisation for Employment (1999) *Standards in Training and Development: A Summary of the Framework and the Qualification Structure*, Employment NTO, Leicester.

Woolfe, R, Murgatroyd, S and Rhys, S (1987) *Guidance and Counselling in Adult and Continuing Education: A Developmental Perspective*, Open University Press, Milton Keynes.

Chapter 20

Conclusions
The significance of the role

In this book we have sought to provide staff developers and other HRD professionals, eg line managers, health and safety officers and welfare officers, with some insight into the HRD and training function and some of the theories of learning. The material is intended to provide a quick reference guide to the practicalities of undertaking various aspects of the training cycle. Information is provided on the qualities needed by staff developers and their career pathways. The terms education and training have been used synonymously, because we are more concerned with learning and the integrity of the individual.

In Part 1 we discussed the basic concepts of how organizations work and emphasized the great extent to which they rely on the expertise of their staff to produce high quality products and services. We emphasized the importance of creating a learning organization and have stressed that often a staff developer's job is determined by the management team. Staff developers have to ensure that their behaviour and ways of working are acceptable to the culture of the organization and that they communicate with the management team, line managers and staff themselves to organize staff development initiatives so as to promote learning in various topics, eg health and safety procedures.

In Part 2 we described the work of staff developers in organizations and listed many roles which could be undertaken. We emphasized that it is virtually impossible for any one training officer to perform all of the jobs or tasks listed. There simply isn't time! Many often specialize or work part time.

We have described the training function and the roles which staff developers undertake. In a learning organization they must undertake many complex social roles so as to ensure that staff development initiatives meet the needs of directors and staff. In most instances they need to remain proactive so as to promote changes of attitude by staff towards the culture of an organization. The job requires a professional approach.

Initiatives for staff development within organizations have gradually evolved from the original simplistic concept of training employees solely to undertake simple tasks competently to the present situation of developing personal, vocational and management skills to enable them to play a complex role within their employing organization. The roles and tasks of staff developers in general are likely to evolve over time, leading to greater specialization and the requirement to update their skills. It is apparent that staff development should remain an ongoing process linked to career development throughout the working life of staff to enable organizations to remain ahead of corporate competition. Indeed, in the present economic situation, it is apparent that opportunities for learning are important factors influencing staff in their willingness to work for organizations in the short or long term.

But staff developers need the support of organizations for funding training programmes and the support of participants not only to take part in the training programmes but also to help their colleagues to learn at the desk or bench. The commitment of staff developers who have a professional approach and who are capable of undertaking many different roles and tasks is also essential. Boundary management has to be undertaken with great care. Staff developers represent catalysts that make the training function 'work'. If they alienate the management team, they lose its support and funding. If they alienate the staff, then the latter may refuse to participate – a balance has to be achieved.

We have seen that, because of the numerous tasks and roles undertaken, the work is often fragmented. The onus is on the staff developer to reduce role overload as far as possible by endeavouring to delegate some of the training roles and tasks to others and to manage time efficiently. In some instances, role conflict is a problem especially where staff developers are working part time and expected to complete a different job as well. Directors and top managers should endeavour to see that role conflict is reduced.

Part 3 of this book is about the practicalities of undertaking the day-to-day running of the training function and the need to follow a training cycle, ie assessing needs, planning and implementing programmes and evaluating the results, then reassessing needs, etc. We have shown that the role of 'Manager of training and development' is particularly complex – a type of balancing act which must be maintained for long periods! We have offered practical advice to make the job easier and the workload lighter where possible.

In Part 4 we provided advice on the presentational, teaching and management skills needed for the job. As discussed in Chapter 19, staff developers need good management skills and the ability to become good leaders. An objective stance has to be achieved. It seems that the attributes and skills of staff developers are often similar to those expected of middle management, eg good communication and interpersonal skills. Other outstanding attributes required include self-confidence in maintaining credibility and the ability to problem-solve.

In summary, we emphasized that all HRD professionals cope with many complex roles. They should seek to update their skills, keeping apace of new developments while managing their own careers as well as those of their colleagues and staff.

In today's society progressive companies need to develop as learning organizations, flexible and responsive to the demands of the global market. The role of staff developers has never been so important to the generation of efficient and proactive companies. Governments are recognizing the importance of training and therefore the role of the staff developer is quite central to future national as well as company development.

Appendix A

Examples of commercial courses

Administration

Executive secretary
Office management

Health and safety

Accidents in the office
First aid
Health education
Risk management
Working with VDUs

Management development

Change management
Computer-based project management
Dealing with conflict
Job shadowing
Managing change
Managing contracts
Managing projects
Motivating people
Organizational change
Project organization

Personal development

Assertiveness
Body language
Communication skills
Dealing with difficult people
Effective decision-making
Interviewing skills
Languages
Presentation skills
Report writing
Stress management
Time management

Quality

Total Quality Management

Running an organization

Appraising staff
Career development
Change agent skills
Employment law
Empowering staff
Environmental management
Equal opportunities
Job evaluation
Negotiating
Organizational communication
Recruitment and selection
Running meetings

Sales and marketing

Customer care
Finance
International marketing
Selling skills

Team-building

Developing teams
Leadership
Team-working

Trainers or instructors

Computer-based training
Counselling
Dealing with people's problems
Facilitating learning
Instructor-led courseware
Skills for trainers
Training the trainer

Appendix B

Some useful addresses

(Web sites or e-mail addresses are given if available)

Australia

Management Advisory Board
Department of Employment, Education, Training and Youth Affairs
GPO Box 9980
Canberra
Act 2701
Australia
Web site: www.detya.gov.au

Canada

Human Resource Development Canada Communications
Place du Portage
Phase IV, 140 Promenade du Portage
Hull PQ K1A OJ9
Canada
E-mail: info@hrdc-drhc.gc.ca

International Council for Adult Education
720 Bathurst Street
Suite 500, Toronto
Ontario, M5S 2R4
Canada
E-mail: icaed@web.cpc.net

Europe

Council of Europe
Documentation centre for Education in Europe
F-67075
Strasbourg, Cedex
E-mail: wilson-barrett@coe.int

European Institute of Education and Social Policy
Universite de Paris
IX - Dauphine
Place du Marechal de Lattre de Tassigney,
F- 75116
Paris
E-mail: ieeps@dauphine.fr

Institute for Development and Adult Education
Chemin August-Vilbert 14
Case Postale 25
CH-1218 Le Grand Sacconex
GE
E-mail: idea@dial.eunet.ch

Organisation for Economic Cooperation and Development
Directorate for labour, Employment and Social Affaires
2 Rue Andre-Pascal
75775 Paris, Cedex 16
France
E-mail: thomas.alexander@oecd.org

Unesco Division of Basic Education
Literacy and Non-formal Education Section
7, Place de Fontenoy
75700 Paris
France
E-mail: literacy@unesco.org

Unesco Institute for Education
Feldbrunnenstrasse 58
D-20148 Hamburg
Germany
E-mail: uie@unesco.org

United Kingdom

Adult Residential Colleges Association (ARCA)
Headlands
Church Lane
Washbrook, Ipswich
Suffolk, IP8 3HF
Web site: www.aredu.demon.co.uk

British Polymer Training Association Ltd
7 Halesfield
Telford TF7 4NA
E-mail: general@bptaserv.co.uk

Careers and Occupational Information Centre
Room W4b
Moorfoot
Sheffield
S. Yorkshire S1 4PQ
E-mail: coic.enqs@dfee.gov.uk

City & Guilds of London Institute (C&G)
1 Giltspur Street,
London ECIA 9DD
E-mail: enquiry@city-and-guilds.co.uk

College of Teachers
Coppice Row
Theydon Bois
Epping CM16 7DN
E-mail: collegeofteachers@mailbox.ulcc.ac.uk

Department for Education and Employment (DfEE)
Sanctuary Buildings
Great Smith Street
London SW1P 3BT
E-mail: info@dfe.gov.uk

EdExcel
Stewart House
32 Russell Square
London WC1B 5DN
E-mail: enquiries@edexcel.org.uk

Engineering and Marine Training Authority (EMTA)
Vector House
41 Clarendon Road
Watford WD1 1HS
Web site: www.emta.org.uk

Institute of Careers Guidance
27a Lower High Street
Stourbridge DY8 1TA
E-mail: hq@icg-uk.org

Institute of Personnel and Development
IPD House
Camp Road
London SW19 4UX
Web site: www.ipd.co.uk

Investors in People UK
7–10 Chandos Street
London W1M 9DE
E-mail: information@iipuk.co.uk

Joint Examining Board
31a Dyer Street
Cirencester
Glos. GL7 2PT
E-mail: jeb@jeb.co.uk

London Chamber of Commerce and Industry Examinations Board
Athena House
112 Station Road
Sidcup
Kent DA15 7BJ
E-mail: custserv@lccieb.org.uk

Management Charter Initiative
Management and Enterprise NTO
Russell Square House
10-12 Russell Square
London WC1B 5BZ
E-mail: mci@compuserve.com

National Assn of Educational Guidance (NAEGA)
1A Hilton Rd
Milngavie
Glasgow G20 8AA
Web site: www.freespace.virgin.net/naega.guidance

National Institute for Adult and Continuing Education
21 De Montford Street
Leicester LEl 7GE
E-mail: enquiries@niace.org.uk

OCR (Oxford Cambridge and RSA Examinations)
Customer Information Bureau
Coventry Office
Progress House
Westwood Way
Coventry CV4 8JQ
E-mail: cib@ocr.org.uk

Open University
Milton Keynes MK7 6AA
Web site: www.open.ac.uk

Open University Validation Services
344–354 Gray's Inn
London WC1X 8BP
E-mail: ouvs-recep@open.ac.uk

Pitman's Qualifications
1 Giltspur Street
London EC1A 9DD
E-mail: abibaker@city-and-guilds.co.uk

Pre-Retirement Association of Great Britain
9 Chesham Rd
Guildford
Surrey GU1 3LS

Qualifications and Curriculum Authority
29 Bolton St
London W1Y 7PD
E-mail: info@qca.org

Scottish Qualifications Authority
Hanover House
24 Douglas Street
Glasgow G2 7NQ
Web site: www.sqa.org.uk

Society for the Advancement of Games and Simulations in Education and
Training (SAGSET)
c/o Peter Walsh
11 Lloyd St, Ryton
Tyne Wear NE40 4DJ
E-mail: peter@j-walsh.freeserve.co.uk

Training and Enterprise National Council
Westminster Tower
3 Albert Embankment
London SE1 7SX
(*see also* local TECs in local directories)

Malaysia

The Secretariat
Headquarters, Ministry of Human Resources
Level 2–4, (B) Block North
Damansara Town Centre
50503 Kuala Lumpur
Malaysia
Web site: www.jaring.my

Director General
Labour Department Malaysia,
Level 5, Block B. Utara, Pusat Bandar Damansara
50532 Kuala Lumpur
Malaysia
E-mail: labdep@po.jaring.my

Singapore

Ministry of Education
Kay Siang Rd
Singapore 1024
Republic of Singapore
E-mail: contact@moe.edu.sg

South America/Caribbean

Unesco Regional Office for Education in Latin America, and the Caribbean
Enrique Delpiano 2058
Casilla 127, Co 29 de Providencia
Santiago
E-mail: ulistg@unesco.org.cl

United States of America

Employment and Training Administration
US Employment Service
200 Constitution Ave
NW 20210, 219-6050
Washington, DC

US Department of Labor
Employment and Training Administration (ETA)
200 Constitution Ave, Room 4700
NW 20210, Washington, DC
E-mail: etapapermaster@doleta.gov

American Society for Training and Development
1640, King St
Box 1443
Alexandria, VA 22313-2043
E-mail: tkim@astd.org

National Association of Workforce Development Professionals
1620 'I' Street, Suite LL30
Washington, DC 20006
E-mail: nawdp@aol.com

National Institute for Work and Learning
Academy for Educational Development
1825 Connecticut Ave. NW
Washington, DC 20009-5721
E-mail: niwl@aed.org

Zimbabwe

Commonwealth Association for the Education and Training of Adults
c/o Department of Adult Education
University of Zimbabwe
Box 167
Mount Pleasant
Harare
Zimbabwe
Web site: www.uz.ac.zw/education/

Appendix C

Types of competency required for National Vocational Qualifications or Scottish Vocational Qualifications for trainers

Sometimes awards are made jointly by two awarding bodies. Some awarding bodies are listed below.

Material in this section was taken from *Standards in Training and Development*, published by the Employment NTO (Department for Education and Employment) (1999) (permission obtained). These standards are now under review prior to Autumn 2001.

Training and Development (Level 3)

The qualification is aimed at those who deliver training and development programmes and those who carry the responsibility for their design and evaluation.

It involves:

Identification of individual learning needs; design of training sessions; preparation of training resources; facilitation of learning through presentation and group activities; evaluation of training and development sessions; evaluation of one's own practice. (10 Units)

Human Resource Development (Level 4)

This qualification is aimed at those candidates who have management responsibility for training and development and are involved in identifying organizational training and development needs and planning the implementation of training and development objectives. They will also be responsible for the improvement of a range of training and development programmes. The award is more concerned with the co-ordination of learning opportunities in line with organizational requirements than the direct delivery of training to individuals or groups.

It involves:

Identification of organizational training needs; devising plans to meet those needs; co-ordinating the provision of learning with others; evaluating and improving training and development programmes; evaluating own practice. (12 Units)

Learning Development (Level 4)

This qualification is aimed at those candidates who are involved in the delivery of learning programmes to individuals or groups. It requires candidates to identify the learning aims, needs and styles of individuals and to design and evaluate programmes to meet those individuals' requirements. The award is more concerned with the facilitation of a broader range of learning opportunities with individuals and groups, rather than the direct instructional training which characterizes that at Level 3.

It involves:

Identifying individuals' learning aims, needs and styles; designing learning programmes to meet learners' aims, needs and styles; agreeing learning programmes with learners; monitoring and reviewing progress with learners; evaluating training programmes; evaluating own practice. (Optional units allow for the inclusion of supporting and advising individual learners, group work and specialist material design, and continuously reviewing and improving training and development methods.) (12 Units)

Training and Development Strategy (Level 5)

The qualification is aimed at those with a strategic responsibility in human resource development, who may either be employed at senior level in an organization or may be a consultant working with organizations at a strategic level. Within the framework of training and development qualifications, those taking level 5 would be setting the policy, direction and context within which those working at levels 3 and 4 would operate. The mandatory units reflect the key characteristics of the occupational area.

It involves:

Identifying organizational human resource requirements, which locates training and development within the wider context of an organization; its development and its overall requirements for human resources; ensuring the strategic position of human resource development within an organisation; complying with professional and ethical requirements; evaluating and developing own practice. (18 Units)

Some awarding bodies

City & Guilds of London Institute (C&G)
EdExcel (formerly BTEC)
Institute of Personnel and Development (IPD)
Joint Examining Board
Open University (OU)
Pitmans Examination Institute
Scottish Vocational Education Council (SCOTVEC)
University of Oxford Delegacy of Local Examinations

Levels of management vocational qualifications developed by the Management Charter Initiative in 1991

Material in this section is taken from the Management Charter Initiative booklet, *What are Management Qualifications?* (1997) (with permission).

Management (Level 3)

This qualification is for practising managers or supervisors who have the following:

a tightly defined area of responsibility; some limited opportunity for taking decisions and managing budgets; responsibility for achieving specific results by using resources effectively; and responsibility for the allocation of work to team members, colleagues or contractors. (7 Units)

Management (Level 4)

This qualification is for practising managers with responsibility for:

allocating work to others; achieving specific results by using resources effectively; carrying out policy in defined areas of authority; controlling limited financial budgets; and contributing to broader activities such as change programmes and recruitment. (9 Units)

Energy Management (Level 4)

This qualification covers the full range of activities expected to be carried out by an Energy Manager and is for either a specialist manager with full or partial responsibility for energy in an organization, or a consultant helping the organization to improve its energy efficiency. (9 Units)

Quality Management (Level 4)

This qualification is either for a specialist manager with responsibility for quality in the organization or a consultant helping the organization to improve its quality performance. (9 Units)

Operational Management (Level 5)

This qualification is for practising managers who:

> have operational responsibility for substantial programmes and resources; have a broad span of control; proactively identify and implement change and quality improvements; negotiate budgets and contracts, and lead high level meetings. (10 Units)

Strategic Management (Level 5)

This qualification is for practising managers who:

> have responsibility for substantial programmes and resources; have responsibility for the strategic development of an organization; have a broad span of control; proactively identify and implement change and quality improvements; negotiate budgets and contracts, and lead high level meetings. (10 Units)

Glossary

The following glossary and abbreviations have been derived from a number of sources including the *MSC Glossary of Training Terms*, (1981) (3rd edn) HMSO, London. Crown copyright is reproduced with the permission of the controller of Her Majesty's Stationery Office.

Action learning Learning through action. . . by individuals. . . a continuous process of learning and reflection, supported by colleagues with the intention of getting things done. (McGill and Beaty, 1992)

Appraisal Assessment of an individual's performance or progress in the exercise of a given assignment or task.

Apprenticeship Any system by which an employer undertakes by contract, to employ a young person and to train her/him for a trade or occupation for a given period of time. Modern apprenticeships may also be government-sponsored.

Audio-visual aids Aids to communication which utilize both sight and hearing, eg videos, films, television, pictures.

Behavioural objectives What a learner is expected to be able to do as a result of training initiatives. (Applies also to job performance objectives.)

Brainstorming A technique used for finding the solutions to problems by means of stimulating ideas from a small group of people. All suggestions are encouraged without criticism and later assessed by the group.

Career development The process of obtaining progressive work experience and training relevant to the way in which people wish to develop. Employers may also promote career development.

Case studies A learning technique in which real or fictional situations are presented to trainees for their analysis and problem-solving.

Coaching A method to increase the experience and ability of trainees by giving them tasks coupled with appraisal, advice and counselling if applicable.

Cognitive skills Skills involved when individuals participate in conscious thought.

Competence Ability to perform a particular activity to a prescribed standard involving a variety of skills.

Computer-assisted learning Involves the use of the computer as a teaching medium or as a learning resource, eg used in the presentation of instructional material.

Computer software Programs which are written in special language to instruct a computer.

Continuing education This relates to the concept that adults should be able to return to education and training as necessary throughout life as a lifetime's supply of appropriate knowledge and skills cannot adequately be provided by school and immediate post-school tuition.

Continuous assessment Assessment of learners at frequent intervals during a course as a complement to, or replacement for, end-of-course examinations.

Core skills Skills central for the achievement of task objectives for any given test as distinct from peripheral skills. Also skills which are crucial to performance of an activity.

Cost-benefit analysis A method of finding the maximum value for a given expenditure.

Counselling A direct relationship in which the counsellor's friendliness, experience and special knowledge are made available to another person.

Culture The taken-for-granted and shared meanings that people assign to their social surroundings.

Curriculum An organized programme of study undertaken in an educational or training-related situation.

Database A structured storage system for data from which it can be retrieved selectively.

Development The growth or realization of a person's ability through learning, often from planned study or experience.

Distance learning A form of learning in which the teachers and course participants are not in the location for most of the course, eg correspondence courses.

E-mail Electronically-transmitted mail.

Enabling objective A statement of what a trainee must be able to do to enable him/her to achieve a desired training objective.

Evaluation of training The assessment of the value of a training system, course or programme in terms of objectives and cost benefits.

Experiential Learning Learning methods developed on the basis that people learn best from reflection and analysis of their experiences.

Faults analysis The process of analysing the faults occurring in a procedure, product or service, specifying the symptoms, causes and remedies of each under headings such as: name of fault, appearance, cause, effect, responsibility, action, prevention.

Feedback Communication about the results of behaviours or attitudes following learning.

Flip chart Large sheets of detachable paper used with felt-tip pens for display (often used during training sessions).

Formal training A structured programme of training by specialist staff.

Health and Safety officer A designated person who is responsible for co-ordination of accident prevention activities and working practices and conditions conducive to health.

Hierarchy of needs A theory of types or levels of human need by individuals (see Maslow 1943, 1954).

Human resources The potential available to an organization from its employees.

Induction Initiatives taken by organizations to familiarize new recruits with their job, ways of working, health and safety procedures, culture, etc of the organization.

Internet Uncentralized world-wide computer network through which information can be accessed.

Interpersonal skills The skills involved in communicating with individuals or within a group while remaining sensitive to their feelings.

Intervention In the context of organization development, the action taken by a third party or change agent in influencing the processes of an organization.

Job The tasks carried out by a particular person for her/his employers.

Job analysis Identification of component tasks required in a given job – often applied to training requirements.

Key roles In the context of training, those roles which are essential to the efficiency of a training system as a whole.

Learning A process of constructing and transforming experience into knowledge, skills, attitudes, values, emotions, senses and beliefs, etc (see definition, Chapter 6).

Lecture A talk given usually by a specialist usually followed by a discussion.

Lesson plan A statement of the main component parts of a lesson laid out in sequence, indicating the methods and techniques to be used and within a given time span.

Management by Objectives (MbO) A technique by which tasks are fixed for individuals over a period of time. Often the outcomes are applied in appraisal reviews.

Management Development Any strategy to promote the effectiveness of managerial staff through planned learning events.

Management succession A system used by an organization which ensures that successive employees are available for management posts.

Mentor A guide, counsellor or advisor of persons with less experience in a particular area of work.

Module Separate units of learning designed as part of a series to lead to a given level of attainment.

Motivate To encourage a course of action or to point out incentives.

National Vocational Qualifications Competence-based job qualifications.

Negative transfer Applies to a learning situation when new learning has not been transferred to the application of a task.

Objectives A statement of the behaviour or skills that a participant is expected to display, eg at the end of a course or lesson.

Off-the-job training Training which normally takes place away from the normal work situation and day-to-day pressures. It may be combined with on-the-job training or further education.

On-the-job training Training given in the normal work situation. Similar to at-the-bench or desk training.

Organization Development Strategies and associated techniques centred on the long-term development of an organization as a whole.

Overhead projector A projector placed in front of the operator which projects transparencies onto a screen behind her/him.

Performance tests The assessment of an individual's performance often used in terms of practical skills.

Positive transfer This applies to a learning situation when newly learned information is successfully transferred to a task.

Programme (As applied to training) units of learning as part of a training initiative.

Programmed instruction A form of instruction which is provided sequentially and determined by an individual learner's needs. Feedback is given as the exercise progresses.

Reinforce To strengthen (learning).

Role How the occupant of a particular position in an organization expects or is expected to behave.

Role conflict The simultaneous existence of two opposing sets of role expectations on a person so that compliance with one makes it difficult to comply with the other.

Role play A learning technique in which students are presented with a situation which they are required to explore by acting out the roles of those represented in this situation.

Simulation The representation of phenomena by equipment or actions, eg by computer models or role play.

Skill An organized and co-ordinated pattern of mental or physical activity in relation to an object, person, event or display of information.

Skills analysis A systematic study of the skills needed to perform a task.

Task Element(s) of work (often applicable to a job).

Task analysis A systematic analysis of the behaviour required to carry out a task with a view to identifying areas of difficulty.

Training A planned process to modify attitude, knowledge or skill behaviour through learning experience to achieve effective performance in an activity or range of activities. In this book it is used synonymously with the term 'education'.

Training function Activity of training within a working organization, ie identification of training needs; the formulation of training objectives; implementation and evaluation of the training process.

Training objective A statement of what a trainee must be able to do at the end of training.

Training programme A schedule of training set out in terms of units of instruction or learning experience often arranged in date sequence and showing the time allowed for each, and broad method of instruction.

Transfer of training The transfer of a previously established or newly learned habit or skill to a task or behaviour (applies often to job training).

Validation 1. Internal validation. A series of tests or assessments designed to ascertain whether a training programme has achieved the objectives specified. 2. External validation. A series of tests and assessments designed to ascertain whether the behavioural objectives of an internally valid training programme were realistically based on an accurate initial identification of training needs in relation to the criteria determined by the organization. 3. It may also be applied to programmed instruction and its effectiveness in helping a target population to learn.

Visual aids These include books, diagrams, flip charts, overhead transparencies, computer simulations. Audio-visual aids include videos and films.

References

Manpower Services Commission (1981) *MSC Glossary of Training Terms*, (3rd edn), HMSO, London.

Maslow, A (1954) *Motivation and Personality*, Harper and Row, New York and London.

McGill, I and Beaty, L (1992) *Action Learning: A Practitioner's Guide*, Kogan Page, London.

Abbreviations

BACIE   British Association for Commercial and Industrial Education
BIM   British Institute of Management
BSI   British Standards Institute
BTEC   Business and Technical Education Council
CAL   Computer-assisted Learning
CBI   Confederation of British Industry
CCTV   Closed Circuit Television
CD ROM   Compact Disk Read-only Memory
CEDEFOP   The European Centre for the Development of Vocational Training
CET   Continuing Education and Training
CGLI   City and Guild of London Institute
CITB   Construction Industry Training Board
CNAA   Council for National Academic Awards
COSHH   Control of Substances Hazardous to Health
CTP   Certificate in Training Practice
DfEE   Department for Education and Employment
EU   European Union
FEU   Further Education Unit
GCSE   General Certificate in Secondary Education
HR   Human Resources
HRD   Human Resource Development
HRM   Human Resource Management
IIP   Investors in People
IPD   Institute of Personnel and Development
IT   Information Technology
LEA   Local Education Authority
LEC   Local Enterprise Council
MbO   Management by Objectives
MCI   Management Charter Initiative
NAEGA   National Association of Educational Guidance for Adults
NGVQ   National General Vocational Qualifications
NIACE   National Institute for Adult and Continuing Education
NTO   National Training Organisation

NVQs National Vocational Qualifications
OD   Organization development
PERT   Programme Evaluation and Review Technique
SVQs   Scottish Vocational Qualifications
TAPs   Training Access Points
TEC   Training and Enterprise Council
TQM   Total Quality Management
VDU   Visual Display Unit
VET   Vocational Education and Training

Author index

Subject index

Visit Kogan Page on-line

Comprehensive information on
Kogan Page titles

Features include

- complete catalogue listings,
  including book reviews and
  descriptions

- special monthly promotions

- information on NEW titles and
  BESTSELLING titles

- a secure shopping basket facility
  for on-line ordering

PLUS everything you need to know
about KOGAN PAGE

http://www.kogan-page.co.uk